Dream Big, Achieve Bigger

Seven Steps to Attract Anything You Want

Tasha L. Mayberry

Dream Big Publishing
ISBN-13: 978-0-692-63592-6

DEDICATION

To our first born son, Vasily, I dedicate this book to you because you created a magical flow of creativity which pushed me to take a dream and make it reality. For years I held the idea for this book close, but it was not until I was pregnant with you just three months along, did the words pour out on paper like a determined, harmonious river. Getting up early in the wee hours of the mornings because of morning sickness (which I've long forgotten because of the beautiful pregnancy I had with you), I would grab my notebook and pen to write while your father was still sleeping. Sitting quietly in perfect harmony as the sun rose up, I wrote each chapter effortlessly. You have brought so much pure joy and love to our lives. Thank you for being our amazing son. I love you. – *Mom*

CONTENTS

	Acknowledgments	1
1	Introduction	Pg 5
2	My Struggle	Pg 19
3	Step 1: Values and Valuing Yourself	Pg 31
4	Step 2: The Power of Positive Thinking	Pg 43
5	Step 3: Gratitude	Pg 51
6	Step 4: Visualization	Pg 61
7	Step 5: Amplifying the Law of Attraction by Taking Action	Pg 77
8	Step 6: Discover Your Passions	Pg 91
9	Step 7: Pay It Forward	Pg 103
10	Final Words	Pg 117

ACKNOWLEDGMENTS

Thank you to my amazing mother, Micheline Mayberry, for teaching me values that built my foundation of honesty, selflessness, gratitude, kindness and great work ethic. You fill my heart with so much pure love; thank you for being the best mom in the universe. Thank you to my entire Mayberry family who have remained unique and colorful (I would not change a thing!) and have shown me unwavering love my entire life. A special thanks to my beautiful sister, Karen Cookson, who has never judged me and continues to inspire and support me.

Further thank you to my dear friend Adriana Tavarez for being my #1 supporter and creative, inspirational, and motivational influencer. From day one your energy has lifted me up. Thank you to Karen Koslov-Barski, the woman, friend, and mother I look up to. I have so much gratitude for you introducing me to "*The Secret*" and setting an example of abundance, kindness, and joy for me and those around you.

Thank you to my amazing book designer, Dennis Hammer, for all that you help with, and a special thank you to my rock star

1

marketing and PR team, Giselle Diaz, Macy Harrell, and Matthew Loftus.

Last, but certainly not least, thank you to my best friend, husband, father of our son. Simply, my soul mate. I'm still amazed by our chance meeting in New York City and now five years married, each day brings such joy that I have never experienced before you. Our journeys together through life will continue to enrich my every day and fill my heart with unconditional love. I love you. Ya lublu tebya.

"Anything you want in life is possible. Just reach out and grab it!"

CHAPTER 1: INTRODUCTION

I'm not a doctor, therapist, or an expert with a degree in what I will teach you—I'm just someone who lost her way and found a path back to an amazing, happy, and abundant life, by following seven simple steps.

Here is where I WAS:

- My life was paralyzed by substance abuse (I was functional at first, but then lost complete control).

- I lived paycheck to paycheck with a bad credit score and no savings (scraping for a dollar to eat lunch at McDonald's some days, and using change to have just enough gas to get to work before payday).

- I was swimming in credit card debt and overdue bills.

- I had self-limiting beliefs and limited confidence.

- I suffered from anxiety and intense panic attacks.

- I was continuously attracting the wrong men/relationships.

- I never seemed to find my true purpose and happiness.

- My life was stagnant.

- I had severe weight fluctuations (I was very thin for many years from not eating much for days at a time, and then became forty pounds overweight from eating out— mostly fast food—for each meal.)

Here is where I am TODAY:

- I am drug-free for over a decade (I am currently thirty-three years old.)

- I am the owner of a six-figure, self-made business (soon to be seven figures).

- I have an excellent credit score over 700 with savings of $20k to $30k consistently in the bank.

- I have ZERO debt aside from my student loans (without ever claiming bankruptcy).

- I am happily married to an amazing husband who is my best friend and biggest supporter.

- I am closing soon on our first home purchase.

- I am eating clean with a healthy lifestyle that I love.

- Exercise is part of my normal routine and I enjoy it; I'm no longer overweight nor have severe weight fluctuations.

- I have no anxiety **without** the use of medications.

- We are having our first baby—it's a boy!

- I know my true self with no limiting beliefs.

- I found my passion and purpose.

- I truly love every minute of life no matter what comes my way.

Seeing the comparison is astounding to me and many of those around me who witnessed my "party days" as a late teen. I often hear how impressed people are at the beautiful person I have become. This is such a nice thing to hear. I owe ALL the changes in my life to the seven steps I will teach you in this book.

Your story may look very different from mine, and that's okay. The beauty of this book is that it's intended to help *anyone*: from those who feel they have hit rock bottom and have no hope, to those who feel like they are losing control and could hit rock bottom, to those who feel stuck and stagnant in life, to those who are happy and successful but want to do and achieve even more—and every other story in between. Whatever your story is, remember that it's your story, and no matter how much "bad" there may be, your story shapes who you are. Although some things in life are not easy and we cannot explain why they happen, I believe everything happens for a reason. The cool part is that we all have the tools to change and achieve more. This book will teach you seven steps to attract anything you want, no matter where you are in life right now. Thank you for taking the time to pick up this book and read it. I am grateful. I want to help. I believe in you.

As I write, I am pregnant with our first baby—very exciting! No one prepared me as a business owner for the morning sickness that comes with this beautiful miracle. I've been sick for the past few weeks, completing the bare minimum for work (something I am not used to, since I love, love, love my work, and most days work twelve-plus hours with complete contentment and joy every minute; this book will help you feel the same). As a result of day-long morning sickness and barely being able to sit up, let alone sit at the computer, work got backed up and funds trickled in slowly (not the norm for our strong business). BUT...I did not lose belief, have doubt, or worry. I knew I would get better, work hard, and make plenty of money to cover expenses. (Payroll for employees is not cheap.) Then all of a sudden, I was better! It felt like a miracle. My morning sickness disappeared for seven days straight. I was able to work like normal and in one week had to make $7K to cover expenses. I did it. I had not a shred of doubt, and this is exactly what I will teach you in this book—how to attract anything you want in life.

The very next week, I was hit with another bout of morning sickness, but again was better a week after this. This time we needed $10K to cover expenses. I don't normally talk about money like this, but will mention examples in this book to show the power of the seven steps I will teach you. This book is all about dreaming big and achieving bigger, and how you can attract not only money, but love, happiness, abundance, success, health, and so much more. So please excuse me up front when I mention money examples in the book (not trying to show off or be rude). But I digress...

Again, to get the $10K we needed, I used the seven steps taught in this book. This may or may not be a lot of money for you or others, but for us, it's a lot of money to make in only a week's time. I've wanted to write this book for years, ever since I changed my life with a simple set of principles—principles that truly turned my life around and sent me soaring to new heights of complete joy, success, abundance, health, love, and more. I was really motivated to write the book by what seemed to be impossible—making $17K in two-and-a-half weeks. (But never once would the thought of something being "impossible" cross my mind. You will learn later how key this is to attracting anything you want.) Time and time again over the years, I've used a simple method to attract anything I want in life. It's worked over and over again. You may be thinking that I'm just lucky—but no, it's not luck. It's all about my thoughts and these seven simple principles that I follow. Once you learn these principles, it will work for you too. I get goose bumps just thinking about it now, and I'm filled with excitement to finally share these steps with you. Something this impactful and life-changing should be shouted from the rooftops! Anyone and everyone can use this book as a guide to dream big and achieve bigger.

The best part of writing this book is helping you and others. My life was not all roses, which I will share about in the coming chapters. If I am able to turn my life around, so are you. And maybe you do not need to necessarily turn your life around. You could already have happiness and love your life but just want to take it to the next level; this book works for that too. So no matter where you are now, once you start to apply these seven steps, you will see change—and we want to hear about it! We set up a Facebook page called "Dream Big, Achieve Bigger" where you can join in on the conversation and share stories of how you used these steps to attract things you dreamed about.

We also wanted to take it a step further and started a non-profit organization called The Dream Fund. A portion of the book proceeds will be donated to The Dream Fund, and we will be awarding grant money to help people achieve their dreams, or at least give them a good start to reach their tallest heights in life. Whether it's $100, $1,000, $10K, or whatever the dollar amount is, visit www.achievebigger.com and apply for a grant. We ask that you share your story and your dream so our team can then choose the grant recipients. The more books we sell, the more grants we can give! We want to help people in a big way and are so excited to have this book printed and in the hands of amazing people like you. Yes, you ARE amazing.

Once you learn these seven steps and activate your internal magnet to attract what you want in life, you will be in complete and utter awe. At least this is how I feel, and still to this day am just astounded by what I am able to achieve by following seven simple steps.

Actually, you are already attracting things in your life right now. Have you ever wanted something really badly, put a lot of energy and focus into it, and made it happen? Or do you wonder why bad things keep coming your way? This is all about attracting everything in your life. If your thoughts are negative or you have limiting beliefs, you will attract bad things and make your limiting beliefs your reality.

This book is to ensure that you attract only the good, positive things you desire in life. Of course, bad things still happen, and there is no way around this—deaths, layoffs, breakups, etc.—but the steps in this book will teach you how to achieve your dreams in a big way and minimize bad occurrences in your life. If something bad happens, the book teaches you how to handle it and quickly turn it around. When bad things happen, you can dwell on it, be angry, say "Why me?" and just create a cycle of negativity that will become your reality. If you are thinking that I am starting to sound a little cuckoo, please keep an open mind. This system works.

I'd also like to mention that this book is not based on religion of any kind, despite my personal beliefs. Although I am a very spiritual person, and believing in a power greater than myself has been monumental in my life, you do not need religion to make these seven steps work for you. I do believe, however, that being spiritual (meaning, believing in a higher power other than yourself in any shape or form you see fit) is important, but I'm not preaching spirituality here. I'm simply and powerfully teaching seven steps to give you the tools to attract what you want in life.

Also, this book is not based on magic. Yes, it's quite a magical feeling to know you have the ability to attract anything you want in life (especially once you start to see results), but it's not magic. It's truly YOU who will dream big and achieve bigger. You, your thoughts, and your deepest beliefs and gratitude are what make these seven steps work.

The concepts taught in this book may seem unbelievable at

times, but to get the most out of this life-changing learning process, remove all thoughts of disbelief. Go all in, and know from this moment forward, YOU WILL believe and achieve. Once you start to experience change and attract the things you want most, it's the most exhilarating feeling. With an open mind to these seven steps, you unlock your inner magnet from within to start to attract all the things you truly dream about. Again, the part that I'm most looking forward to is all the stories I will hear after you and others start using my seven-step system. (I don't really want to say "my" system; it's "our" system, really.) To get things started, here are some examples from my life of how I attracted great things.

I went to this amazing conference called "Spark & Hustle" hosted by Tory Johnson. (I'm not sure if she still does these, but if so, I highly recommend you attend if you are a woman.) I was still working full-time in my corporate career and had started a PR/marketing side business. Take note that I said "side business" for something to come later. We did one small exercise at the conference that changed the trajectory of my business and life. We were asked to write down three numbers to answer these questions:

1. How much money do you make monthly?
2. How much are your monthly expenses?
3. How much do you want to make each month?

I've worked since the age of fourteen, if memory serves me (the earliest I was able to work legally), sometimes working three jobs to pay my way through college. Through the years, I always lived paycheck to paycheck, until I was almost thirty years old. Now that I have developed this seven-step system, I recognize a factor as to why I was living like that. Each pay period, I would always set a budget, writing down how much money I received from my paycheck(s) and how many expenses I had during that pay period. I thought I was budgeting—which technically I was—but I never thought to write down how much money I WANTED to make. This is the missing key. Later in the book, I will explain why.

At the conference, I wrote down something like:

1. $3,000: monthly revenue
2. $2,000: monthly expenses
3. $10,000: how much I want to make each month

Within three months of writing down that I wanted to make $10K a month, we went from $3K a month to $10K a month. (I say "we" because I own a business with my husband.) Again, I was raised with manners and would not normally discuss money like this, but I am sharing all of this to illustrate examples in my life where I followed the principles in this book to attract what I truly wanted.

Back when I did this exercise—probably four or more years ago—I did not have the seven-step system securely in place. But by then, I was already a strong believer and practitioner of The Secret. Before I attended the Spark & Hustle conference, I would listen to the audio book during my two-hour daily commute to work. This was truly the turning point in my life that set me on a path to greatness, happiness, and abundance. Listen to or read this book; I highly recommend it. I perfected and added to the concepts that Rhonda Byrne taught me in *The Secret*, creating a seven-step system that you will learn in the next several chapters.

Another reason we went from $3K a month to $10K a month is that I stopped calling my business a "side" business. Every day, I would go through my gratitude list (which is one of the steps you will learn about later) and I kept saying, "I am so grateful our side business is successful." At the time, I was working as the vice president of marketing and public relations in the corporate world. (This is another example of me attracting what I wanted, even before I knew I was using the principles in this book. I will share more later on.) So our PR/marketing firm was our business on the side. But in my thoughts, side business meant a business on the side that brings in some supplemental income. I say "in my thoughts" because everything I attract is based on my own thoughts and beliefs. If I thought a side business meant a successful part-time business that brings in a ton of money, then this would be different; I would attract exactly this. But I truly thought of side business as a non-primary job that brings in some supplemental income—enough to help out, and that's it.

Wait a minute…Is this what I really wanted? Is this what I was really grateful for? Yes, a business on the side that brings in supplemental income is still amazing. But for me, I truly wanted to only work for myself and flourish in success. So this was not a side business after all.

Every day after I realized my thoughts, I changed my thinking/gratitude list in part by saying, "I am so grateful for our successful business." One subtle change in thought—simply removing the word "side"—made all the difference in what I was attracting. Now in my new thought process, "successful" meant helping a ton of people while making a lot of dough. So this is exactly what I attracted.

Within three months of changing my thoughts—essentially recognizing my true dream and goal—and wanting to make $10K per month, not only were we bringing in $10K a month, but my corporate nine-to-five career ended and I was my own boss. It was amazing...but it didn't stop there.

I did the three-number exercise I learned at the conference again and again. Each time we met the new goal of how much we wanted to make in a month, we would set a new goal. Within six months, we were earning six figures. My dreams were coming true. This is when I started to think, "Geesh, I should write a book so other people can do this too!" I felt like I was my own magician, creating reality and achieving my dreams and goals. But I am no magician. I am just following a simple set of steps that you will learn in this book to activate your internal magnet to attract what you truly want in life.

There are many more examples that I will share in the coming chapters.

So here we are. Before we move on to the next chapter, I want to thank you so much for investing your precious time in reading my book. I wrote this book with no fluff; it's very to-the-point so the reading is easy and you get the most out of it. The seven steps you will learn will help you in many more ways than just making your dreams a reality and even achieving bigger than your dreams. The system will help you be the best you, the happiest you, and just an overall decent and good person. Use this book to attract love, friendship, success, wealth, joy, abundance, health—everything you want from all facets of life.

Once you unlock your inner magnet, you will feel in control of your life—like you can do anything you want and truly be happy no matter what comes your way. This feeling is almost indescribable—as I will say often because it's the only way to truly describe it—and is the reason I love life. You will feel all these great things too, and even if you already love life at this moment, you will elevate that feeling even more. As I said, this book is for everyone. Those who feel they've hit rock bottom (a feeling I am too familiar with and will share more on later), those who feel stuck or stagnant in life, those who are happy with their life and want to achieve more, and anyone in between. I am on the edge of my seat to share with you the seven steps. But first, it was not always all roses for me...

"Your past does not define you. It shapes you into a beautiful butterfly if you always look forward, embrace positive change, and do the next right thing."

CHAPTER 2: MY STRUGGLE

You will learn many things about me, since my life is a great example of how to truly attract anything you want in life no matter how bad things may be. I want to be honest with you about the personal struggles I have gone through to show that turning your life around, no matter who or where you are, is possible, even at the darkest point. I know that some people reading this book have experienced even darker days than I have; this book will help even the worst of the worst. Anything is possible.

One important fact that I have learned to truly believe is that my past is my past—it does NOT define me. If I did not learn the concepts I teach in this book, I honestly believe that I would not be able to open up about the things I've gone through. But my struggles made me the person I am today, and I am in such a different place that it's truly enlightening. I'm more grateful than words can begin to describe for going from where I was to where I am now. I vowed to never bury or forget my struggles, but instead to know that they happened and that I pulled through by taking action to change. If you want something bad enough, you just have to reach out and grab it.

So here's my story…

I was raised by an amazing single mother in a small town called Windham, Maine. (If you have not visited Maine, I highly recommend it. Portland, Old Orchard Beach, and Sebago Lake in Windham are all must-see places in Maine. I'm a Maine native and have not ventured to even a quarter of the state). I did not grow up with a full-time father; there were some occasional weekend nights spent with him when I was young, but these trickled to a halt by the time I was a teenager. As a child and teenager, I thought it did not bother me or impact me, but I realized the affect it had on me many years later. I felt embarrassed that I came from a broken family and dreamed of having siblings and two parents. Today, I have ZERO embarrassment and have learned that I am who I am today because I was raised by my amazing mother. And when I say amazing mom, I mean AMAZING. I never went without. My mom worked three jobs—a corporate day job at Unum and two part-time jobs in retail and banquets. My mom taught me the best values in the best way: through her actions—hard work, honesty, selflessness, generosity, and kindness.

One summer when I was five years old and we were between homes, we stayed in a tiny, mint-green camper in the backyard of my mom's best friend's farmhouse. We were invited to stay inside the house, but my mom's friend already had a family of five, plus my mom always wanted to figure it out on her own. She accepted the offer to stay in the camper in the backyard. It was for one summer and I do not remember much, but this is an example of my mom making things happen. We had shelter, we were warm, we used the shower and bathroom in the farmhouse, we had food, and we had each other. It wasn't ideal or our first choice, of course, but it was the only good choice at the time, and we were okay with this temporary fix until we moved into a new home (which we did once the summer was over). Growing up, I always knew everything would be okay because of my mom. I learned survival from her. Years later, my mom married and built a new home where I grew up as a teenager. This is when I took some wrong turns.

During my teen years, I fell into substance abuse. Marijuana in Maine was (and still is) very common; even adults smoked pot. They didn't do it directly in front of me, but I knew what was going on. At an early age, I started drinking and smoking pot. My mom was working a lot, which gave me a lot of freedom. I maintained A's in school, always did my homework, and was a good teen—so I am not even sure my mom knew I was abusing substances in the beginning. I started hanging with the "cool" party group. It was a lot of fun but led me down roads better not traveled. As I reflect back now, I see the progression of my substance abuse and all the wrong turns I took. But I do not dwell on my bad choices as I once did; this only keeps me stuck in my past and I am only about today and the future. Again, my past does not define me—a true, inner belief I know now. It's very liberating.

As I mentioned, I got good grades in honors classes at school and my mom never had to harp on me to do my homework. I enjoyed doing well in school, and it came very easy to me, earning A's and B's without much studying and hardly ever reading a book. I see Facebook posts now from the other smart girls who were in my classes, and if I knew then what I know now, I would have befriended these girls. But I cannot change my past, so I don't think about this much. The best thing I can do now is teach my future children what I have learned in life.

As a rebellious teen, the occasional partying escalated as the years went on, causing me to venture into some dark places in my late teen years. Most of the time, I remained in college, worked, and was functional. But all of this eventually ended and I found myself with no job, no home, no communication with my family, and just having no real life. Substance abuse took over my life. I was slowly killing myself. Today, when I look back, I know by the grace of God and my guardian angels that I was saved. Not saved in a religious sense, but just saved from a continued life of drugs and downward spiral. I am petrified by the thought that I could have ended up dead or in jail—especially because it would have destroyed my mother. Those teen years spent partying seem like another galaxy compared to where I am today.

I've been clean for ten years, maybe even more—I've lost count! I value life so much more and know how precious it truly is. Ever since I was a little girl, I wanted to do great things. I always dreamed of being a business women and traveling, since we did not have the means to travel growing up—except for one big family trip to Disney when I was nine. Addiction can happen to anyone. With all my dreams, ambition, and a great upbringing, I was still caught up in the vicious cycle.

I remember one Thanksgiving when I found myself at an apartment in New Hampshire belonging to someone I barely knew. I often found myself in unfamiliar places after an all-night rave party. While he and his father went out for Thanksgiving dinner, I stayed behind alone. That day, I ate one Reese's Peanut Butter Cup; coming from a family that gathered together for a feast each year, this was heartbreaking. Shame filled my heart. I thought about how worried my mother must be. But the addiction had such a hold on me that even this did not lead me to change.

There was another time that my mom showed up at my apartment with the police to bring me to rehab. Outside my door, my mom pleaded with me to pack a bag and go get help. She was desperate to help me. My heart breaks writing these words, thinking of the pain and worry my mom was going through. I was still not ready for change. I did not answer her or open the door, and because I was eighteen, the police could not do anything. There was eventually silence outside my door, and I continued on my destructive path.

Less than two years later, while I was living in a party house after getting evicted from my apartment, my mom dropped off a letter and a photo of her and me when I was a baby. At this time, I hadn't seen my mom in about seven months; before, I would see her every day. This hit me like a ton of bricks. My addiction had buried my emotions for years. But deep inside, my mom knew she could reach me and she never gave up. I looked around and thought to myself, "Is this it? All my dreams have faded and I am wasting away. What am I doing?" At that very moment, as I read my mom's letter and tears fell on the photograph of her and me as a baby, I started the slow transition to a clean, drug-free life. But it took a very scary occurrence to wake me up completely.

I was in a hotel with a friend when a couple other guys who we thought were friends came in and robbed us. One of them choked me, and, being an asthmatic, I was beyond scared. Instead of being angry at the two guys who did this, I actually owe them my life and gratitude because after this, things began to change for me. Before, it was just hanging out partying with friends, but being physically assaulted and robbed was a scary thing—too scary for me. I had never been involved in a life of crime, stealing, or anything like this during my battle with addiction. I wanted no part of that type of life—as assailant or victim.

After this happened to me, I took drastic measures to take my life back. Whatever it took, I was willing to do it. I immediately moved back in with my mom and checked into rehab. It was not easy, but I did it. After two inpatient stays at rehab and two intense out-patient rehab programs, I was living a clean life. I learned so much about myself in rehab. I am not ashamed to share that I went to rehab. My counselor said that I was like a beautiful butterfly that transformed from the time I arrived to the time I left. These words have stuck with me all these years.

My life was changed forever. I was ready to dream again and make my mom proud. I wanted a life I deserved—a life of happiness and fulfillment. Tears come to my eyes as I write this chapter. Reliving the experience is difficult, but if my story can help just one other person find their way back, it's worth the flood of emotions I am feeling now. I know many people who know me today will probably be in disbelief that I went through this experience. I am hopeful that I will not be judged, as this is my story and I believe sharing it will only lead to helping others. This is all I want.

In my twenties, I did a lot of soul searching. I uncovered buried feelings from my childhood and teen years and began to process everything. I grew so much as a person during these years. Around age twenty-five, a dear friend of mine, Karen Barski (the most beautiful person I know), told me about *The Secret*, an amazing book by Rhonda Byrne. This would become my true turning point, but I did not read the book right away because I was in a toxic relationship at the time. When I was finally on my own again, I could focus on me, my happiness, and my life. At age twenty-seven, I listened to the audio book version. At that very point, I realized that I had been using the "secret" concept already to attract things I wanted in life without even knowing it. But after I read the book, I was equipped with even more knowledge. I felt empowered.

I've always been the type of person to believe I can do anything—very ambitious. Growing up in Maine, my mom and I would go to the Maine Mall—basically the only good mall in Maine. While driving back home on the highway, we would pass the giant Unum insurance building where my mom worked. As we passed the enormous building, I would turn my head, point my finger up, and say, "Mom, I'm going to work there when I grow up."

Sure enough, at only twenty-one years old, I landed a career at Unum as a long-term disability benefits specialist. I wanted it. I envisioned it as a little girl. I believed it. It happened. There's even a second part to landing this career of a lifetime. Right out of college, I had a two-year degree in Paralegal Studies and began working at a law firm. I used the principles I teach in this book to land that job. I went in to be interviewed for the receptionist position, but I believed and wanted to be hired as a legal assistant. During the interview, they said they were so impressed, that they wanted to hire me as a legal assistant. But back to the Unum story…

So at age twenty, right out of college, I worked as a legal assistant in a law firm. It was an amazing personal injury firm called Lowry & Associates. It was an incredible experience, but I was not making enough money—typical me: reaching for the stars and wanting more. Unum was hiring, but everyone wants to work at Unum in Maine since it really is THE best place to work in our area. With so many wanting to get in, it's not easy to be hired or even get an interview. They even have a three-part interview process: phone interview, computer testing, and face-to-face interview with three "higher-ups."

At the time, I wanted to make $40K a year. I was making $21K at the law firm. So I started my search and found a posting for Unum at $40K a year! I applied, was chosen to be interviewed, and went through the stringent interview process. I remember doing the initial phone interview on my lunch break in the parking lot of a Panera Bread. Finally, I heard back from them that I was hired! So even back then, I was using the basic principles I teach in this book but without consciously knowing it. Just like you are doing now, only perhaps you are just attracting the wrong things because of your thoughts and beliefs.

At twenty-two, I was very proud and thought I was happy and in love. I met someone, and in eight months, he proposed. I thought for sure he was the one…but there was another plan for me.

My mom and stepfather were about to put the non-refundable deposit on the ballroom where the wedding reception would take place. But the wedding never happened.

Driving the forty-five minutes home from Unum one day, my then-fiancé called me and said that we needed to talk. All the way home, I had a funny feeling in my stomach, wondering what this meant. As far as I knew, everything was going well. There was no warning for what happened next.

When I walked in the house, my ex-fiancé was sitting on the couch. I do not remember his exact words, but I remember the look on his face—stone cold and very serious. He basically said that he was moving out and the wedding was off. I stood in disbelief. Was I hearing this for real? Was I stuck in a bad nightmare? Is this some type of joke—no, it was not April Fool's Day. How can we go from happy and normal to this?

He then proceeded to pack his bag and left right then and there to stay with friends down the street. I was on my knees crying and praying that this was not happening. I didn't understand at the time, but now it's crystal, crystal clear.

I was meant to meet my current husband—my best friend, my soul mate, the father of my son. When I reflect back on the pain I went through, I did not understand why at the time. But now I do. So I carry this life lesson with me, and every time something happens that is not favorable, I know there must be a reason. This prevents me from getting super upset, dwelling on things, or worrying. Even for small things like blowing past an exit on the highway and having to double back ten minutes to get to the right exit. No need to get upset; this may have happened so as to avoid an accident or something. You just never know the reason, but trust there is one.

It's funny, though, that three months after my ex-fiancé left, after I had moved on was already in my own apartment, he came knocking on my door wanting to get back together. By then, it was way too late, and I am glad I did not go back. I needed to meet my true match.

Before I met my husband, I had a boyfriend who moved to Connecticut for the summer…and I followed. This was eight years ago and I'm still in Connecticut. It's funny how things happen; if I had never moved to Connecticut, I would have never met my amazing husband in New York City.

While in Connecticut, I enrolled in college to get my Bachelor's and started working as a paralegal. I was eventually laid off when the market crashed and was out of work for over a year. This made me think what else I was good at and liked to do. I always loved to write and be creative, so I switched gears into social media marketing. Marketing was (and is) my true passion. Shortly after, I was hired to handle the marketing and public relations for an insurance brokerage firm. I excelled so much that in four months, they promoted me to vice president of marketing and public relations. I had not read *The Secret* yet and didn't know about the steps I teach in this book, but I knew what I wanted and was already attracting them.

I even used these steps to find love. After being in an unhealthy relationship, I tried internet dating—lots of dates, but no love. It wasn't until I started focusing on myself that I knew the type of man I wanted to meet. I went to the gym, worked hard, and with confidence, I thought and believed the exact type of man I wanted to meet—and it happened. By chance, after a networking event in New York City, I met my husband. Today, we are best friends and have been married for five years with our first baby on the way!

As I close this chapter, I remind you that it's always good to remember and not be ashamed of where you came from. Even the bad things that happen in life mold us into who we are as individuals. I see it as two choices:

You can feel ashamed, disappointed, angry, or resentful for any bad things that happened, or

You can recognize it, process it, learn from it, and do the next right thing. Own it as your past but know that it does not define you.

"You ARE worth it. No matter where you've been or where you are. You have a purpose."

CHAPTER 3: STEP 1—VALUES AND VALUING YOURSELF

I am a true believer that good things happen to good people. Karma is real. Those who always think or say, "Good guys finish last," will attract this. The universe is a powerful force that listens to us, especially our innermost thoughts and beliefs. The basis for this concept is the law of attraction, which we will get into later on in more detail, the gist of which is what you think and believe (what you project), is what you will attract.

Now, if you say or think things like the following, you will attract exactly the things you do not want: I'm so broke, I'll never pay off my debt, I will never get a raise, I can't find a good woman or man, I don't want to gain weight, etc. (By the way, the universe does not hear or process the words "don't," "not," and "no." Therefore, "I don't want to gain weight" is really you saying, "I want to gain weight.")

31

Now that you know a little more about how our thoughts affect what we attract, we can move on. Values play a big role in creating a solid foundation to achieving our dreams, so in part, Step 1 is about your core values. Unfortunately, I cannot teach you good values; these depend on your own moral compass. For me, I was shown (not taught, but shown through my mom's actions) values such as generosity, selflessness, honesty, great work ethic, doing good even when no one is looking, and a desire to genuinely want to help others. These values are my foundation, and with a strong foundation, the next six steps are easier.

I am so grateful to have the best mom in the world. But I first have to talk about and give credit to my dearest Meme, my late grandmother. When Meme passed, just before Christmas in 2014, heaven gained and angel for sure. My grandmother met my grandfather during World War II on the French Riviera. It was a whirlwind romance, and Meme found herself crossing the big Atlantic Ocean to America. She married my grandfather and settled in Windham, Maine, a town where our family is the second settlers. She was quite shocked upon arrival. The town of Windham today is quite developed, but back then, it was a simple country town. The nearest city was Portland, Maine— thirty minutes away. Meme went from the great city of Paris— where she wore the latest fashion trends, dined at Parisian cafes, and walked daily to the market to buy the freshest breads, cheeses, and more—to now being in a small country town in Maine. It was a culture shock, to say the least.

Not knowing any English, Meme taught herself the language from the radio and a dictionary. This is just one example of my grandmother's determination, will, and strength. She went on to have five children: my mom, my two aunts, and my two uncles. They all grew up on the Mayberry Farm, growing their own food only a field away from my mom's grandparents' house. Although married to my Meme and living at the farmhouse, my grandfather was not around much, so my meme raised all five children essentially on her own. Plus, she always worked. She passed down her strong work ethic, generosity, selflessness, strength, and more to her five children, and then my mom passed them to me.

I just had to mention my angel of a grandmother—a beautiful, caring soul, so kind and gentle. She kept her French accent until the end and even spoke fluent French before the dementia set in. Meme was our family's foundation—a fountain of good values and morals that spilled over to each generation and a fountain that will continue on to my children. Even though I was the first family member to attend college, all my aunts and uncles own their own businesses. Meme did well. I love you my, Meme. J'taime forever.

Worksheet #1

Sit quietly for a moment and write down all the values that are important to you. Use these as your foundation to ground you.

Values Important to Me

1. _____

2. _____

3. _____

4. _____

5. _____

6. _____

7. _____

8. _____

9. _____

10. _____

Here's the biggest part of Step 1:

Valuing yourself.

Have you ever heard someone say, "You cannot love and make someone else happy until you love yourself and make yourself happy?" Well, this is true. Personally, I made mistakes in my teens and spent many years of my twenties finding my true self. Now, at age thirty-three, I have a true sense of purpose and respect for myself. I value myself greatly. This is not being conceited; this is being healthy. And I know I am still learning about myself and growing. It's an amazing place to be in life, and I attribute this to the seven steps I teach in this book.

My point in sharing all of this is to show that YOU are the most important person to value. Even as a parent, you must hold yourself in high regard and value yourself. As a result, you will be a better parent. This does not mean putting yourself ahead of your kids. Instead, I mean to know, think, and truly believe you are valuable. You have a purpose. No matter your past, you are worth it. And once you have value for yourself, you can then believe in yourself and dream BIG. A good friend once told me that the world is my oyster—so I decided to make pearls!

It's easy to self-doubt and have limiting beliefs. I had many myself that I did not even know I had until I really took a step back and reflected on my true, innermost voice. Growing up, I thought, believed, and said, "I cannot run the mile in gym class because I have asthma." So I would get a doctor's note for the gym teacher and walk it every time for all the years I was in school. This then led me to believe, "I cannot play sports because I have asthma." So I didn't play sports. Later, during college, I started to jog at the gym. I remember I slowly did five minutes, walked twenty, and so on. After a few weeks went by, I was jogging for forty minutes straight without needing my inhaler medicine. I took one puff before I started and I was good to go. I was so proud, and thought all these years I did not put value on what my body is capable of despite my asthma. This is an example of how our thoughts affect our reality and dictate our actions.

Growing up, I also thought that because I came from a broken family, I was less desirable to be friends with. In school, I had my group of friends and knew other kids, but I never befriended the "smart girls" who were in my honors classes (except for my best friend, Carrie Rickett). There were probably many reasons for these limiting beliefs: "I'm too different because I only have a mom." "We don't like the same things." "They won't like me." "They won't accept me." Now I see some of these girls from my classes on Facebook and we have so much in common! All those limiting beliefs prevented me from making more amazing, life-long friends. But I don't dwell on thoughts of should-have, could-have. This is merely an observation that I am sharing for the book. Dwelling on the past with what-ifs or I-should-haves doesn't help move your life forward. This just keeps you stuck in the past, rehashing and reliving what happened and creating major roadblocks for your internal magnet, which is used to attract what you truly want in life. So, be in the moment and always look forward.

Okay, so back to valuing yourself. Once this is accomplished, then you can truly believe in yourself. This may not be easy at first, but after practicing these seven steps, you will be your biggest cheerleader. And again, this is not conceit, as that brings negative energy. You need to believe in yourself in a healthy, confident way. You truly can do anything you want. Never forget this, and never let anyone else make you think differently. You have a lot to offer. You are worth it!

I have a whiteboard next to my desk, and each day, I write, "Today I can and I will." I heard this from Gina Rodriguez from Jane the Virgin, accepting her Golden Globe award in 2015. She said, "My father used to tell me to say every morning 'Today is going to be a great today. I can and I will.' Well, Dad, today is a great day. I can and I did." This is a way for me to remind myself each day to believe that I can make anything happen.

Worksheet #2

Step 1: Take a piece of paper (one that you will rip up eventually when instructed) and write down all your limiting beliefs. Dig deep inside and be honest.

Step 2: In the spaces you see on the next page, change each limiting belief into a positive statement—the opposite of your limiting belief.

So if your original statement is, "I don't know anything about business so I cannot start my own successful business," change it to something like, "I can and will start my own business, and it does not matter if I have any formal business training because I am a self-learner. There are a ton of books and online resources, and I can make anything happen."

Or another example: Your limiting belief is, "I will never meet the right man or woman," or "All the good men/women are taken," or "I hope to meet the right man/woman." (The last one is a bit more positive than the others, but could still be stronger. The word "hope" insinuates that it's not happening and you hope there is a chance it will. I avoid using the word hope in my thoughts and always make my thoughts more definitive.) Change these statements to something like, "The man/woman of my dreams will come into my life and make me very happy," or "I will attract my soul mate and fall in love."

Another example: If you think, "I cannot afford to pay off debt. I can barely stay afloat on current bills," change it to, "I will pay off my debt in X year(s). I will have the extra money to clear my debt."

My Positive Statements

1. _____

2. _____

3. _____

4. _____

5. _____

6. _____

7. _____

8. _____

9. _____

10. _____

Step 3: Rip up the piece of paper that you wrote your limiting beliefs on. Focus now on your new, positive beliefs. Yes, it could take time to truly believe your new positive statements, but remove all self-doubt and don't lose focus.

I will warn you now that some people that don't know about or understand the principles in this book *may* say negative things at first. Don't get frustrated; it's okay that they have their own opinion, and it does not have to affect you or your thoughts. The cool part is that once they start seeing change and witness you attracting all these great things, they will start to be more curious and want to learn the power of these seven steps. This happened with my dear husband.

My husband is a self-proclaimed "realist." This is fairly common among Russians, and there is nothing wrong with it. But when I initially told my husband about *The Secret* (after listening to the audio book), he was skeptical. When certain circumstances would normally stress people out, I would reply, "Everything will work out. Let's will it to happen." He would say, "You are living in a pink world." Yes, I am living in a pink world because I choose to live positively with everything around me. If something bad comes my way, I choose to follow these seven steps to attract the outcome I want. Instead of getting defensive or letting his comments bother me, I just stayed positive and continued with the steps. Again, everyone has the right to their own opinion, and we shouldn't push beliefs on people.

So with that said, just know that there could be naysayers; but again, everyone has the right to say what they believe and think. As you start attracting happiness, success, wealth, love, and abundance by following these seven steps, you feel such inner self-control and accomplishment—just pure joy that you made it happen. You will feel like telling everyone about how you are attracting everything you want in life; this is a good thing, as you will learn in Step 7 about paying it forward. Just be prepared because everyone receives ideas differently. Some will be hesitant to believe, but most everyone in my experience is eager to hear and learn more. My best advice is to just respect the reaction no matter what, don't let anyone affect what you believe, and by all means, do not let anyone get you thinking any limiting beliefs about yourself. Only YOU have the power to let negative people affect you. Just listen and it's best not to even argue back. With my husband, I kept quiet, continued with these seven steps, and showed him through actions the results over the past five or more years. The best part is that now he understands the principles taught in this book and believes they work! He is even starting to use these steps himself—even if it's quietly.

Overall, Step 1 is meant to build your foundation of values, truly value yourself, and know you have a purpose no matter what happened in the past or what is happening right now in your life. You are worth it. Once you've accomplished these things, start to believe. Truly believe you can attract and do anything you want in life. Erasing self-doubt may not be easy for everyone, but once you master it, it's an amazing state to be in. Some of you reading this book could be ahead of the game and already have Step 1 complete. This book is for all walks of life and will apply to people differently. But no matter who you are, knowing and believing you can achieve anything is quite magical.

"Manifesting and making our dreams our reality starts with our thoughts and true, inner beliefs."

CHAPTER 4: STEP 2—THE POWER OF POSITIVE THINKING

Our thoughts affect and control our emotions, actions, and what we attract in life. Our thoughts are very powerful. Step 2 is a crucial step in the seven-step process of awakening your internal magnet within in order to attract everything you want in life. Positive thinking may not be easy at first, but with practice you will find yourself thinking only positively no matter what comes your way. This is so liberating and, for me, is the best feeling in the world—to know that no matter what happens, I will think positively. I am human, though, and on rare occasions, I will catch myself thinking negatively for a moment. But it's so amazing that I've retrained my brain to immediately identify a negative, toxic thought and correct it quickly. This happens instantaneously for me now.

By conquering Step 2, my life has transformed into beautiful joy and peace. It's almost indescribable. I was not a negative person by nature before. But after some reflection, I found many toxic, negative thoughts that were hindering what I truly wanted to attract in life—thoughts like:

- My credit score is so bad.

- I have so much school loan debt.

- I don't want to gain weight.

- I have the worst stomach.

- I hate my butt and wish it were toned.

- I attract all the wrong men.

- I need to make my paycheck last until next pay period.

- I have social anxiety and it's hard for me to make new, quality friends.

- I am damaged because of my past with addiction.

- Good, family-oriented men won't love me because I was raised by a single mom.

- I'm so ashamed of my party past.

The list goes on and on. Until I learned about limiting beliefs and positive thinking, I did not even know that these thoughts were blocking my internal magnet from attracting the true things I wanted in life. I had to dig some of these thoughts out from deep down inside. It was like a cleansing process in a way. I needed to identify my negative thoughts and limiting beliefs so I could then turn them around. This is similar to the exercise you did in Step 1.

When I look back at these thoughts, I understand now why I was attracting everything I actually did not want in life. Because of these thoughts, I attracted what I was thinking. If I wanted to attract the right man, then I needed to start thinking, "I am so grateful that I met the man of my dreams and am so happy!" Even if this did not happen yet, think and feel as if it has to attract exactly this. We will go over gratitude more in a later step.

For years, I said I could not afford to pay my student loans. By thinking and believing this, I was attracting exactly this to my life. A beautiful thing happened when I first learned the concepts in this book. I changed all my negative thoughts and any thoughts with a limiting belief and started to see drastic, positive changes in my life. Words cannot describe how my life, my entire being, and my person changed when I simply started thinking positively.

So instead I started thinking things like:

- I am so excited that my credit score is above 700.

- I am able to afford to pay toward my student loan debt each month. Feels great!

- I am healthy, strong, and fit.

- I love my toned body.

- I attract men who respect me and treat me right.

- I have more than enough money in my bank.

- I feel confident in social settings and attract new, quality friends easily.

- My past with addiction does not define me; it made me the strong women I am today. With my story, I will help others who are suffering. I have no shame.

- My husband will love me, especially because I was raised by a single mom who passed down her amazing strength to me.

With just changing my thoughts around to be positive, and truly believing each thought as if it already happened, I was able to accomplish:

- Having a credit score over 700 after having bad credit for over ten years of my life.

- Making monthly payments on my student loans.

- Eating clean and exercising as part of my lifestyle.

- Maintaining a healthy weight—at one point, losing forty pounds.

- Not living paycheck to paycheck any longer and owning a self-made business that makes six figures.

- Being 100% comfortable in social settings or networking events, talking with anyone and making friends/connections. I don't even think I have social anxiety anymore.

- Having NO shame for my past with addiction. This was

not easy to overcome, but feels amazing now! I am willing to share my story to help others find their way.

- Meeting my husband by chance in New York City. We have been married for five years with our first baby on the way. My husband does not blink an eye about me being raised without my father. His parents are still married after many years and he has never discounted me because I was raised by a single parent. He actually told me that thinking that he would even care about this is very silly.

- And much more!

Many people will spend night and day worrying, which only magnifies the problem. Instead, re-structure your thoughts, believe them, and know you will solve the problem at hand. This has worked for me time and time again for years. I've proven the philosophy and these steps truly work.

It takes practice, but we all have the ability to retrain our thoughts, and be aware of all negative thoughts as soon as they pop in our minds. Something as simple as thinking, "Ugh! Monday again" can be changed to "It's Monday! A new, fresh start of the week! This week I will be productive and accomplish so much." This one change in thought can turn your entire week around – and especially make your Monday better.

Thoughts like "The job market is so bad right now; I cannot find any decent work" actually works negatively against what you really want to achieve: getting a job. Instead, re-structure your thought to something like, "The job market is getting better and I am so grateful I found the perfect job!" Even though this may not have happened yet, thoughts like this strengthen your internal magnet. We will touch on this more in the next chapter.

Worksheet #3

Write a list of negative or limiting thoughts. You may not even realize you were thinking negatively until you do this exercise. Even thoughts like, "My child never goes to bed easily" are limiting beliefs. You think this, you attract this.

Negative, Limiting Thoughts	My New Positive Thoughts and Beliefs

"The more gratitude you have, the more things you will attract to be grateful for."

CHAPTER 5: STEP 4—GRATITUDE

No matter where you are in life at this very moment, there is always something or something more to be grateful for. We will talk more about the law of attraction in chapter seven, but one thing is very true, real, and amazing to experience:

The more gratitude you have, the more you will attract things in your life to be grateful for.

You may be asking, "How can I be grateful if I am broke, sick, homeless, cannot find work, or always hitting dead-ends?" This can pertain to whatever else that is going on in your life that is difficult to deal with.

I say this is the best time to show gratitude to turn things around. Self-pity and being angry at the world creates gigantic roadblocks for your internal magnet.

I am grateful for many things, but the small things matter most; this is exactly how I started. I am grateful for putting two feet on the ground when I get up each day. Heck, I am grateful

51

for waking up and having another day in this life. I am grateful for the air that I breathe. I'm grateful for my family. I am even grateful that I know and understand gratitude and the seven steps in this book. If you want more things to be grateful for, showing daily gratitude is a powerful way to make this happen.

There are many ways to show gratitude. A friend, Diane Lang—an amazing positive living expert and coach with great books too—calls it "daily gratitude checks." Meaning you go through a list of things you are grateful for each day and by doing so, you boost your happiness. Plus, having gratitude aligns you with more amazing things to be grateful for.

Every morning when I wake up, I brush my teeth with one of those Sonicare toothbrushes with a two-minute timer. As I brush my teeth I go through my gratitude list in my head. I think of everything from small things to big, including things that have not happened yet. For each thing, I say, "I am so grateful for XXXXX." Once I go through my entire list, I say a thank you for each gratitude check I listed and think of each item again that I'm grateful for in my head.

The key to this exercise is saying your gratitude list and giving thanks with complete conviction and with a smile inside your mind, like you are thanking the universe and showing pure and true gratitude. I feel excitement as I do this exercise; I'm excited for all the things I have accomplished and will accomplish. This is my favorite way to start each day. It puts me in a positive frame of mind and reminds me of how far I have come and of all the great things I want to attract to go even further in this beautiful life.

My husband and I still live in a small studio condo in a high rise. It's very cozy, with no big closet or storage space. Living here over our past five years together, we are running out of room and it seems that things are piling up everywhere. Yes, I could complain, saying and thinking things like, "I don't want to live in a small place." But thinking these kinds of thoughts won't help us get into a bigger home. In fact, this thinking will prevent us from moving; remember, the universe removes the word "don't" and hears me say, "I want to live in a small place." So instead, I have gratitude for the studio condo we live in. I'm grateful it's our own place, we have a roof over our heads, we have the means to pay the rent each month, and my husband and I have grown so close being in such a small place. I'm grateful for the pool, the parking garage, the building's gym, the twenty-four-hour security desk, and the list goes on.

Being grateful for things we have—even if it's not exactly what we want—does something magical. It opens the universe to help us get into a bigger home. Some people would worry about what they were going to do with such a small condo with a baby due in only a few months. But worrying does not activate your inner magnet to attract what you want. Worrying does the exact opposite and can manifest what you are hoping doesn't happen. We know that by April, we will be in a bigger home, and I add this to my daily gratitude list. My beautiful sister calls this a "grateful intention."

As an example, when I'm going through my gratitude list each morning I say things like:

- I am so grateful to be in our new, three-bedroom home

we bought before the baby was born.

- I am so grateful my asthma is symptom-free.

- I am so grateful I lost ten pounds. (I am pregnant now so I leave this one out these days.)

- I am so grateful we have a new, smart, amazing employee.

All of these are grateful intentions—things that I am grateful for that have not happened yet. This is the key to attracting anything you want in life. Yes, be grateful for things in the present and this will help you attract more things to be grateful for. But adding gratitude for things that will happen later is powerful as well.

When you say or think your grateful intentions, you must believe as if it happened already without a shred of doubt. Feel the joy and other emotions as if your grateful intention has already become real. When you think it, believe it, and act as if it already happened, you are sending signals to the universe to more easily make these dreams comes true. Once you experience this process, it's almost indescribable to know that you can attract anything you want in life. One day, as you go through your gratitude list, you will realize that your grateful intentions are now current realities to be grateful for. It's awesome.

Another thing I do is visualize my grateful intentions as I say them. This helps evoke real feelings as if it happened. Later on, we will talk more about visualization.

Sometimes, when I am at the gym stretching after a workout, I will lie on my back, shut my eyes, and go through my gratitude list for a second time that day. I do this when my body is at its optimal relaxation and peak focus. So whatever makes you relaxed and focused, try doing your gratitude list at that time. I love doing my list in the mornings because right when I get up, I'm not flooded with thoughts for the day or work. I'm just waking up, so my mind is clear. When your mind is clear, the universe can hear your thoughts better.

Another great time I do my gratitude list is when I am lying in bed before sleep. But before I finish my list, I always fall fast asleep; this is okay though, since I already did my entire list in the morning. I believe starting and ending the day with gratitude makes your inner magnet stronger. It's like you are creating a positive container for your entire day—beginning and end.

When driving alone in the car, I listen to jazz. But I often find myself turning the music off, praying, then doing my gratitude list. You can do your gratitude check as many times as you want in a day, but once a day in a focused state is sufficient. Gratitude goes beyond feeling thankful. It's a deep feeling of appreciation.

Worksheet #4

What are you grateful for presently?	What are your grateful intentions?

As I shared before, I grew up in the amazing state of Maine. I never went without but was not handed everything either. Living in Maine and being raised by a single mom really prepared me for appreciating everything that came my way. I was fortunate to have been taught gratitude growing up.

When I first moved to Connecticut, I stayed with a boyfriend's aunt. We would use couch pillows to make a bed in the living room of the small, trendy, one-bedroom apartment. We stayed there for three or four months, and I remember being so grateful to have that space on the floor to sleep, a roof over my head, smoothies, delicious food, and great company. It was all I needed. I was taking online college courses and eventually started working at a fantastic law firm in Norwalk, Connecticut called DePanfilis and Vallerie. My boyfriend and I then got our own place in Bridgeport, Connecticut. It was a studio apartment in the South End of Bridgeport; most people would be nervous even driving in this area let alone living there. It was a far cry from his aunt's trendy place, my mom's home, and my previous apartments in Maine, but regardless, I was so grateful. I was surrounded by culture and made the best of it.

So, I was living in this small studio above a busy store in the South End. Three blocks to the right was the beautiful campus of the University of Bridgeport and Seaside Park, and one block to the left of us were the projects. My mom visited Connecticut once while I lived there, but I did not show her the apartment; that's how bad it was. But again, I was still grateful. I felt safe because we knew all the neighbors, and we came to find out that people in those communities look out for one another which I really liked. Even though I was not living in my ideal apartment or neighborhood, I had a job at a law firm, I had my own SUV, and air in my lungs. Back then, I was not practicing these seven steps and had not learned about the principles I teach in this book. But I recall always having some gratitude no matter where I was in life. It's a trait that I have to thank my mother for.

Today, however, I know gratitude in a different, more powerful way. I was so excited to write this chapter because I truly believe having gratitude is the basis of my happiness. Gratitude has made me so happy and grateful intentions have come true over and over again. Seeing these steps work is the most amazing feeling. When you start to see change, we want to hear from you!

Life is so short. It sounds cliché, but it's true. In seven years, I will be forty years old with a six-year-old child. It seems like yesterday I was in my late teens/early twenties trying to find my way. But at the same time, it feels like a world away because of the stark difference in my life between then and now.

Gratitude helps me be in the moment and realize all the good in my life. Yes, there is so much more I will accomplish, but gratitude helps me keep the good things in my mind and not dwell or worry about the bad.

I recently added to my daily gratitude list:

- I am so grateful I had a smooth, healthy, and happy pregnancy.

- I am grateful I had a smooth, healthy labor.

- I am so grateful our baby is smart, healthy, and beautiful.

I'm only three-and-a-half months pregnant as I write this chapter, but I am thinking, believing, and envisioning all of these things to have already happened and to be true. (Note: as I proofread this chapter, I am seven months pregnant and have had a smooth pregnancy so far.)

Many moms, especially first time moms-to-be, worry about whether they can handle labor or if their baby will be healthy; these are normal thoughts and feelings. Instead, I focus on grateful intentions to attract what I want. This helps me remove fear, too.

Energy is powerful. Our thoughts and our entire being are all energy. I feel so empowered to be able to channel positive thoughts, beliefs, and gratitude to attract what I want in life—and now you can too.

I am excited to share the steps with you. By following this system, you will see amazing changes in your life. I'm beyond excited to release this book and start hearing stories of success. My motivation behind this book is to help people, and the rewarding part is hearing your stories.

With that said, I will close by saying I am grateful for you—grateful you found this book and are taking your precious time to read my story and these seven steps.

"Visualize your dreams as detailed as possible while feeling emotions as if it already happened. This makes your internal magnet strong."

CHAPTER 6: STEP 3— VISUALIZATION

All successful people consciously or subconsciously use visualization to attract things in life. Again, this is not magic, although it seems quite magical once you start visualizing what you want and your dreams and thoughts become reality.

Visualization is very powerful and is a key step; I know I say this about all the steps, but each step plays such an important role. We all are beings of energy that make up the universe. So our thoughts—especially vivid, emotion-filled, focused thoughts—can alter our environment, events, and more. It's quite empowering to know that we all have the ability to activate our internal magnet and through simple visualization, dream big and achieve bigger.

I personally use visualization every day. When I go through my gratitude list and especially when I think of my grateful intentions, I visualize each. So when I say, "I'm so grateful to be living in our first home we purchased before our baby was born," I not only believe it has already happened and feel emotions as if it happened, I visualize the house with as much detail as possible. I even search on the internet for houses as if I was buying one right now. Seeing the homes I like helps me visualize better. Taking steps toward your dream helps to attract it to you faster. Want a new car? Start browsing online or go to a dealership to look. Want to go on vacation? Start looking online and start planning where you want to go and when. Want to receive more money? Fill out a deposit slip from your bank with the amount of money you want to attract. (Hold on to it, of course, but the process of you filling out the deposit slip is taking steps toward your dream.) We will talk more about the law of attraction and taking action later on.

I use visualization for work a lot too. I visualize each day to maximize my productivity. There is an excellent productivity worksheet created by Brendon Burchard. If you have not heard of Brendon Burchard, I highly recommend his book, *The Charge*, and his total product blueprint course. Here is a link to his 1-Page Productivity Planner: http://www.highperformanceacademy.com/HPA-1pageproductivity.pdf. I fill this out each morning, and once complete, I visualize each item and think of a successful, productive, positive day.

I especially use visualization before each client call or meeting. If it's a new prospective client, I visualize myself closing the deal or whatever outcome I want to happen. I even visualize before vacation! I think of what we will do, how I will relax and take it all in, how we'll have a safe flight, and more. Looking online for photos of where we will be vacationing helps create more vivid visualizations.

Receiving my first $10,000 check in the mail was also based on visualization. All my life, I lived paycheck to paycheck. By following these seven steps, I made a complete turnaround toward true financial independence. Receiving the check was a big deal for me. I remember days I would have to scrape change to get gas or a dollar or two to eat lunch from the McDonald's dollar menu until payday came. So to visualize and manifest a $10K check was surreal to say the least.

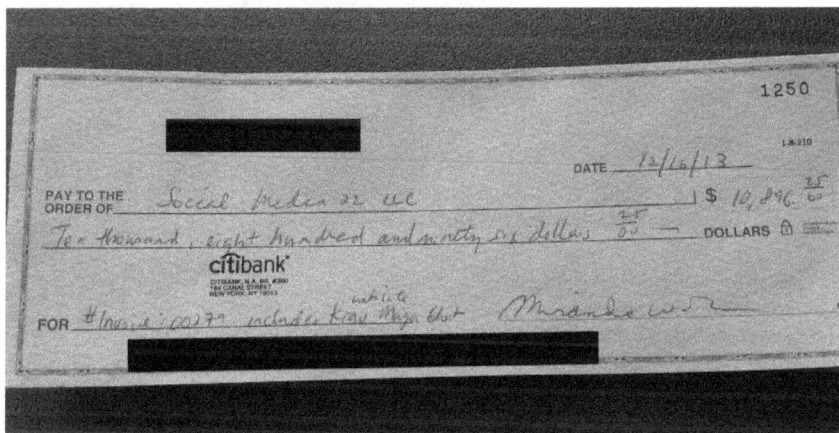

I used to say I wanted to keep a constant $20K in our bank after all expenses were paid each month. I visualized this and it came true. One day, I realized that I had been limiting us by thinking this way. So I changed my thinking and started visualizing $30K in the bank. Within two weeks, we hit $33K.

Be sure to catch any limiting beliefs when you visualize what you want to attract. Of course, I was extremely grateful to always have expenses paid and $20K in the bank, but why stop there?

Here's an example, if you are living in a small apartment or living with your parents, maybe you feel frustrated and stuck or you have no extra money to move up. These thoughts are hard not to focus on. But because these are your thoughts, this is what you will continue to attract. Instead, be grateful for the roof over your head and visualize yourself in your ideal home with extra money. Keep thinking and believing that without a doubt, living in your ideal place with money in your wallet IS your reality and you will be amazed at how things turn around.

Here are three steps to make visualization more effective:

Step 1: Think of what you want with as many details as possible. You want to buy your first house? Visualize signing the papers at the bank, getting keys to your new house, walking in your home, etc. Think about what that home will look like and who you are celebrating with.

Step 2: Feel emotions as if what you are visualizing has already happened. You could think, "Someday I will buy a house," but this is limiting. It's not totally bad, but you can take it a step further to strengthen your internal magnet to attract what you want faster. Instead, say, "I'm so excited we bought our first home." Then feel as if it already happened. Feel gratitude, happiness, joy, accomplishment—any feelings associated with owning your own home. Smile when you visualize it.

Step 3: Believe without a doubt. Even with our best intentions to think positively, we all have an inner voice that can doubt our thoughts. You must transform your innermost voice and remove all doubt. This goes back to Step 1: valuing yourself, knowing you are worth it, and knowing that you can make anything happen. You can and will do anything you believe.

I used to have positive thoughts about losing weight. But I realized that my internal voice, deep down, would be saying, "It's hard for me to lose these last ten pounds," or "I am in my thirties now and my metabolism is not what it used to be." So even though I was visualizing losing ten pounds, my inner voice was still holding me back. It wasn't until I removed all doubts and limiting beliefs that I was able to break past the barrier and the last ten pounds. This process takes time and is not always easy. Most of our deepest thoughts come from when we grew up or from painful experiences. After years of thinking these things—even if we do not realize we are doing it—we believe them, and it will take more than a day to remove these beliefs. So be patient!

Once you recognize your limiting beliefs, you can then visualize clearly and have a strong internal magnet to attract the things you want in life. When you catch your inner voice combatting against your positive thoughts, visualize a little person deep inside you. Visualize yourself picking up that little inner voice and turning it upside down, shaking out all those limiting beliefs. Then say, "I can and I will. My positive thoughts are strong. My negative thoughts are weak. My inner voice has no doubts."

You can visualize however you want; the little person inside is just one way, but you can choose whatever works best for you and your process. This is the beauty of visualization. Sound a little kooky? Maybe—but it works. There is no right or wrong way to visualize; I have found that following the three steps previously outlined will help you visualize more effectively.

There is a story I wanted to share that is connected to visualization:

I had a marvelous, uplifting, and feel-good conversation with a woman named Marla—famously known as "The Fly Lady." She has written amazing books that I highly recommend. We were talking one day and she shared a lovely story with me about Saint Therese. Neither of us are Catholic, but the story of Saint Therese is touching.

Saint Therese was a nun at the early age of fifteen, even though the age requirement was eighteen. When she was just fourteen years old, she took a pilgrimage to Rome and was able to visit and talk with Pope Leo XIII. She approached the pope, knelt, and asked him to allow her to enter Carmel Convent at the age of fifteen.

She always did everything with love. She was bullied in the convent, but still gave love in return and never complained as she did all the menial chores that others did not want to do. "What matters in life," she wrote, "is not great deeds, but great love." (http://www.littleflower.org/therese/) Therese lived and taught a spirituality of attending to everyone and everything well and with love. Saint Therese's life was cut short by tuberculosis at the age of twenty-four. She became a saint because of her unwavering kindness, love, and dedication to God.

Marla told me an amazing story about her experience

visiting the Saint Therese Shrine in Darien, Illinois. Marla was writing her new book—actually taking a break from writing for our phone call—in which she shares her beautiful experience.

She also told me that if you pray to Saint Therese, a rose will show up in the coming days. So one night, as I was doing dishes, I quietly prayed to Saint Therese. I am not religious, per say; I do believe in God, I'm a Christian, and have been baptized, but I like to say that I am spiritual as opposed to religious. My prayer went something like this:

"Hello, Saint Therese. I heard your beautiful story and pray to you now to thank you for setting an example. I pray that I exude the qualities of kindness you showed to others. If you hear me, let me see a rose. Amen."

The very next day, my husband and I went out to lunch and searched online for a place nearby to vacuum and clean the inside of the car. We found a place close to the restaurant, but and as I approached the driveway, I didn't turn in; I kept going. My husband asked me why I didn't turn in. I replied, "Not sure. Can you check for another self-wash or vacuum place?" We found another one on the way home and I drove by this one too! I said to my husband, "Let's just go to that gas station near our house and use their vacuum machine."

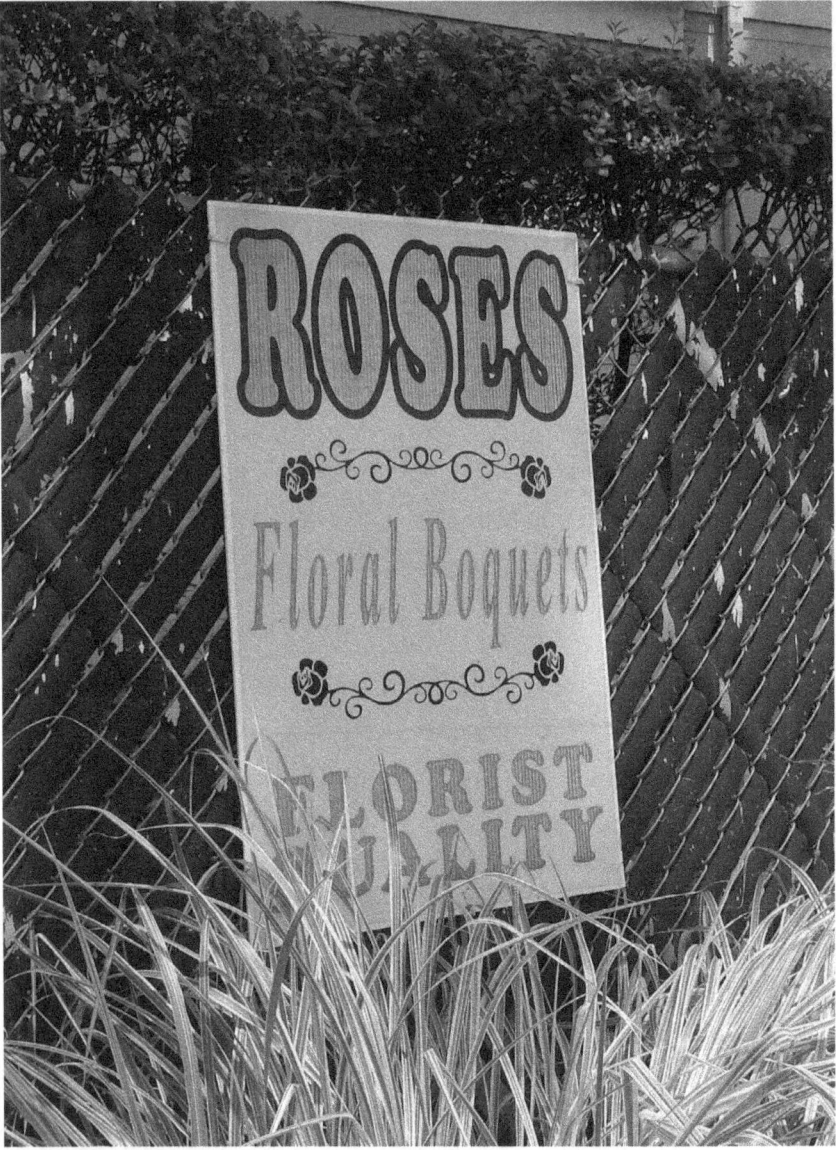

We pulled into the gas station, carefully parked the car close enough to the vacuum, and started to clean. Then I noticed something really cool; there was a large sign on the fence near the vacuum console with roses on it! I smiled from ear to ear.

68

The sign is gone now, but I snapped a photo of the sign to send to Marla.

Perhaps it was Saint Therese showing me the rose, or it could be the fact that I visualized seeing a rose, believing I truly would see one after praying to Saint Therese and I attracted this to me. Either way, it was magical.

The book that I am always raving about, *The Secret*, does an exercise where you visualize a feather—the look, the color, any other detail—and then you see it. I tried this once and visualized a white feather; within a week, I had a white feather stuck on my jacket.

Visualization truly works. By following the three steps to effective visualization that I mentioned earlier in the chapter, you get into the habit and it becomes second nature. Another exercise I learned from The Secret is when you receive bills in the mail, add a zero at the end and visualize that the bills you receive are actually checks you are receiving. Visualize money coming in instead of money you have to pay out. Truly feel that the bill you are holding is money you are receiving. This will help attract money to you. It's really neat, and when it starts working, it's truly amazing.

Another excellent tool to help you visualize is a vision board. I make a vision board each year, and it's truly amazing to see everything come true. I first learned about vision boards from my dear friend Karen Barski, who I mentioned earlier in the book. Karen did a family vision board when she first started her baby swaddle business, Woombie.com. On the vision board were things like a mansion, a million-dollar check made out to her from the universe, and more. Today, she has it all, including a multi-million-dollar brand.

Last February, my best friend, Adriana, and I made vision boards together at the library. We bought big, white poster board paper and other materials. When we got to the library, we found a large table that was perfect to spread our materials out on. We brought a ton of old magazines with us, so we each started browsing through them, cutting our words, letters, shapes, and photos that we felt connected to. Then we assembled and glued our creations on our visions boards!

Here is my vision board:

My best friend, Adriana's, vision board.

Here are all the things that came true in 2015 from my vision board: the house came in early 2016 and is under contract currently…closing soon! The new car will be after the house, since we were advised not to buy a new car before getting a mortgage.

(see next page)

I organized my vision board in a certain way, intentionally adding a house, new car, and kids last at the bottom. I envisioned everything else to come first in the year, and then the house, new car, and kids later on—maybe even in 2016. But the universe had a different plan. Be careful what you put on your vision board! We unexpectedly (without trying) got pregnant in July, 2015—not even five months after I created my vision board! We are so delighted about our baby.

Adriana added a guitar on her vision board to represent her learning to play. Two weeks later, her boss unexpectedly gave her a guitar for free! Just thinking about it gives me goose bumps.

The main thing to take away from Step 4 (visualization) is to not only think and believe what you want to attract to yourself, but visualize it as well. Want to meet the perfect woman or man? Visualize what they look like, see yourselves going on dates together, and even getting married. Want a raise? Visualize your boss giving you a raise. Truly see how that would look—being called into his/her office or the boss stopping by your office to tell you the news. Trying to find a new job? Visualize your dream job; see yourself sending in your resume and cover letter, getting a phone call to go on an interview, going to the interview and doing great, getting a call back with an offer, your first day at work, etc. When visualizing, remember to believe what you are attracting to yourself. Have no doubts—know that it will happen.

Worksheet #5

Write details for everything you want to attract and how you will visualize it.

Things I Want to Attract Most in Life

1. _____

2. _____

3. _____

4. _____

5. _____

6. _____

7. _____

8. _____

9. _____

10. _____

Start visualizing each!

This is a perfect lead-in to Step 5— Amplifying Law of Attraction by Taking Action.

"What you think, believe and project is what you attract. Take action towards every dream big or small."

CHAPTER 7: STEP 5—AMPLIFYING THE LAW OF ATTRACTION BY TAKING ACTION

Wikipedia says it well: "The law of attraction is the name given to the maxim 'like attracts like,' which, in New Thought philosophy, is used to sum up the idea that by focusing on positive or negative thoughts, a person brings positive or negative experiences into their life."

(https://en.wikipedia.org/wiki/Law_of_attraction_%28New_Thought%29)

I used to say, "I always attract bad boys." And you know what happened? I continued to attract all the wrong men. It wasn't until I changed my thoughts, true inner voice, and beliefs to, "I met an amazing husband and am so happy," that I attracted exactly this.

Remember, your true thoughts and beliefs can be something you want, but has not happened yet. In my experience, when you think of these wants in life, phrasing it as if it already happened and feeling the emotions that are associated with it already being your reality is heard louder by the universe. Yes, you could say, "I will meet an amazing husband/wife and be so happy." This is not totally bad, but changing it to, "I met an amazing husband/wife…" is even stronger. It may feel a little strange at first to think and believe things that have not happened yet, but this feeling will dissipate quickly once you start attracting everything you want in life and it truly becomes your reality.

Another example that I mentioned earlier is that I used to think, "I have social anxiety and people won't like me." Thinking back now, this is a terrible, self-limiting belief that consumed me for years. I was confident to a certain extent, but this was my deep inner voice which dictated social situations. Of course, I was still social and had friends, but I was held back in many ways, now that I look back. This self-limiting belief even made me think that I needed a glass of wine in a social setting to warm up to people. This could not be further from the truth. I haven't had a sip of alcohol for months now during my pregnancy and have been in business and social settings where I had an amazing time talking with new people.

Before, when I had this limited belief deep inside, I would shy away from meeting new people. Now I think AND believe, "I am a confident, amazing women, wife, and friend. I attract new growth friends and people see me for me—my true, authentic, amazing self. I empower others around me to feel the same energy. I enjoy meeting new people and having a positive effect on those in my life. I attract good people in my life." I believe EVERY word of this, and every word continuously comes true. This is my true inner voice now and this is what I attract. This is the law of attraction. My whole sense of self-purpose and confidence has transformed. I grew into a beautiful butterfly, and I've never been so happy, so fulfilled, and so sure of myself and my life. I'm excited to grow even more, which I undoubtedly will, since I'm only thirty-three years old.

(As a side note, a "growth friend" is a friend that supports, inspires, and encourages you. Essentially, helping you grow as a person. I learned this from Brendon Burchard and he has a video about three types of friends that I found very helpful: https://www.youtube.com/watch?v=Ir0w3VPVi5Q)

By following these seven steps, you too can feel everything I experience, plus more. I always say, "If you want something, reach out and grab it." After learning and practicing the principles taught in this book, you truly feel like you can achieve anything. It all starts with dreaming big; don't limit yourself. Then use these steps to manifest exactly what you want. You do have to put the work in, of course. I did not create a six-figure business by just wishful thinking. Like I said before, these steps are not intended to make all good things magically appear in your life (although it can feel like this). It also takes action.

In everything I attracted, I took action: working hard, long hours for our business, eating clean and working out, paying off debt to get a good credit score, etc. You cannot just think positively, have gratitude, visualize what you want, and sit back waiting for it all to come to you. There may be some things you will attract without much action—it has happened to me. But mostly, you will need to actively work toward achieving your dreams, especially if you want them to manifest quickly.

Taking action can be done for small things too. For example, if you want to buy a new home but won't be ready until next year, you can still take action now to start attracting the purchase of a home. Start browsing homes online and save the ones you like. Calculate how much you can borrow using online mortgage calculators. Start talking about buying a home with friends and family. Even meet with a mortgage broker to see what steps are needed to buy a house. These actions leading up to the purchase will make it a lot easier to attract your new home. I know some people that wouldn't take any of these actions because they do not have the money to buy a home right now. If you think like this, you will never buy a home, or when you do buy a home, you could have purchased it a lot sooner. You are thinking and believing, "I do not have money to buy a home." So you will attract exactly that. Change this thought to, "I am so grateful and excited we bought a home." Then do small actions to start the process. It's okay if you don't have a dime in the bank to buy a home. The actions you take, your thoughts, and your beliefs will lead you to where you want to be.

You want to get a great job? Brush up on your interviewing and resume-writing skills, look on job boards daily and apply to positions, meet with a recruiter or coach to further help you, go buy a great outfit for your interviews, etc. Take action to make your dream a reality.

You want to be clean and sober? This takes a lot of action, but you can break free. Actively seek help: rehab, outpatient programs, lean on family, and reconnect with those who truly love you and will be there for you. Take it a step further; cleanse your life of any negative people, especially those who are using. If they are friends, this may be more difficult, but it's a must. Surround yourself with positive people full of life, even if this is just family or one good friend to start. If you don't have positive family or friends, then attend AA or NA; meetings are full of positive influences.

You want a happy marriage? In addition to thinking positively, believing and knowing what you want, having gratitude, and visualizing happiness, take action. Start communicating with your spouse or partner. Talk about what makes you unhappy, listen to what makes them unhappy, and discuss how each person can change. Take baby steps at first. Just talking about it is a huge first step. It's not always easy, but it feels great to be on the same page together. You married for a reason. Think back to your first days and what you loved about your other half. Reminiscing is something I do often to remind myself just how grateful I am to have my husband, my true match and best friend. Do small acts of affection and make time for date night. Giving a compliment or saying "I love you" goes a long way too. Surprise your better half by doing the dishes or cooking dinner. All these actions will amplify the law of attraction. I am a believer in working hard, so I worked toward everything I want in life—and my dreams are coming true.

You want to lose weight? Action is required. Write down a small weight loss goal to start—even if it's only five pounds.

Start eating clean Monday through Friday and allow a treat or two on the weekends. Start walking, going to the gym, or doing a short workout DVD at home. Even the busiest person can find time to exercise thirty minutes a day. Most of all, rid your thoughts and deep inner voice of all those limiting beliefs: I have no time to work out, I have too much to lose, it will take forever, I cannot afford the gym, etc. Action makes our dreams become reality. Yes, the steps in this book attract what we want to us quickly, but we also have the responsibility to work toward each of our goals.

I even use the law of attraction and specific action steps to get rid of my anxiety. I used to suffer with anxiety and get panic attacks; these are not fun. One time, driving through North Windham in Maine, I had a severe panic attack. I had to pull over at my doctor's office and sit in their waiting room sipping water until it passed, which took over an hour. Another time, after some stress at the Danbury, Connecticut DMV, I returned to my office and had severe anxiety. I had to lie on the office couch as my co-workers talked me through it. After almost two hours, I was able to drive home. Today, I use these seven steps to overcome my anxiety. I no longer have panic attacks and very minimal anxiety that lasts seconds or minutes. I also don't take anxiety medications and never have because I feel that natural is best—exercise, positive thinking, etc.

When anxiety tries to creep up and hit me, I immediately recognize it as anxiety. I no longer feel like I am dying with racing thoughts of a having a heart attack, stroke, or brain aneurism. For me, my anxiety comes with physical symptoms of arm tingling, neck tightness, etc., so my mind always thought the worse, which made my anxiety worse. So when I feel like my arm is tingly and/or my neck is getting tight on one side, I know this is just my anxiety trying to get me. So I take some deep breaths and say aloud to someone, "I'm feeling anxiety but I know it will pass quickly. I'll drink some water so it will go away." While I say this, I truly believe it. I am not fearful like I used to be when a panic attack or anxiety started. Something about saying out loud that I am feeling anxiety quickly helps me get over it. Maybe it's the comfort of letting someone else know this is what I am feeling or maybe it's feeling empowered knowing that this is anxiety and I won't let it get the best of me. Either way, when I tell someone these words, I truly believe and visualize my anxiety going away. I drink a glass of water and think to myself, "By the time I drink this full glass of water, I will have no anxiety." Within minutes, it's gone—sometimes within seconds. No panic attack. No prolonged hours of anxiety and feeling like I am going to die. No medication. This took practice, of course, but it became easier and easier each time.

When I go through my daily gratitude list, I say, "I am so grateful that my anxiety is gone." This has helped tremendously. My anxiety may creep up a few times a year instead of multiple times a week like it used to. But when it does come, I know how to focus and help dissipate the feelings.

Having anxiety is not fun, and many people use drugs or alcohol to help suppress the symptoms, but really I think it makes it worse. I am NOT A DOCTOR and this is NOT medical advice. I'm just sharing my personal experience and story on how I use these seven steps to overcome my anxiety. I believe that others can do the same, but everyone is different so I can only speak on how I handle my anxiety. Some people may need medication, and that's up to them and their doctor.

A funny little side note: my husband is from Russia and we visit my in-laws in his home city once or twice a year. Russians do not know the word "anxiety." I'm not sure if the medical doctors do or not, but the people of Russia do not know this word. As a result, they do not suffer with anxiety. I cannot speak for the entire country of Russia, but in our big circle of friends and family, everyone we asked does not know the word or the feeling. I think this is interesting and backs up the theory that what we don't know or believe cannot manifest. Of course, this is not a sure thing, but generally speaking, I personally believe this. I think it's quite interesting.

As another example of this theory, I do not read anything negative while pregnant—negative labor stories, negative stories about pregnancy complications, etc. If someone starts telling me a pregnancy horror story, I kindly stop them and tell them I'd rather not know. Instead, I have focused on the positive: the stages and growth of our baby, eating clean, drinking one hundred ounces of water a day, taking my prenatal vitamins, exercising, being happy, limiting and eliminating stress, reading stories of empowerment, singing to my unborn son, and visualizing a healthy pregnancy, delivery, and baby. For me, personally, I do not want to read about all the things that could go wrong. If I know about them and think about them, I could attract these negative things to me.

I do think education is important so you are prepared, but I see no need in filling your head with everything bad that COULD happen. I am definitely not saying to ever ignore symptoms that you may experience and that thinking positively will make everything okay. It's important to seek medical attention if you feel something is off or wrong.

Overall, the law of attraction is a beautiful concept. What you project, think, and believe is what you attract to yourself. This is just the first part, though. Taking action will bring everything full circle and make your internal magnet much stronger. I'm excited to hear your stories of how it works for you!

I wrote this book to help people. I want this book in the hands of teenagers, college students, young adults entering the world, people dealing with substance abuse, people in prison, entrepreneurs who are dreaming big, CEOs, parents, and really everyone from any walk of life. Even if you feel like you have it all or have nothing at all with no chance to change, this book is for you too.

I truly believe in each of these seven steps with my entire being. These steps have made me a better person, a better wife, a better friend, a better business owner, a better leader, and soon, a better mom. After reading this book, you will have the tools and ability to attract everything you want in life. This process—these steps—don't discriminate.

As I handwrite this chapter today, it's Friday the thirteenth. This is an interesting day. Some people say and believe today is unlucky and bad things will happen. The key is they believe this to be true. Call it superstitious, but if they believe it, they will attract exactly this. I personally believe Friday the thirteenth is a lucky day and great things will happen. Every Friday the thirteenth for me, good things happen. This is the law of attraction.

One time, my husband and I tested the law of attraction before going to the Hollywood Casino in Ft. Lauderdale. We wrote on a hotel napkin, "We are so happy we won $500!" As I wrote on the napkin, my true inner thoughts were, "$500 is a lot to win; I'd be happy with at least $250." So we went to the casino, which was a rare occurrence for us since my husband dislikes gambling—but it was our honeymoon, so we went for it. We played the slots and walked out with $250! It was amazing.

We never tried this again, and I'm not recommending that you use these steps to gamble because the house always wins no matter how hard you believe, visualize, and want to attract winnings. I shared the story because I wrote $500, but my true inner thought was winning $250—and we won just that. So it goes to show you that you could have surface thoughts with great intentions, but you should listen to your inner voice and make sure it aligns with your dreams and wants.

I believe that people that go into situations truly believing they will succeed will achieve more times than not. For example, you could have a big presentation and think one of two ways:

I'm dreading this presentation I have to do. I'm terrible at public speaking. I probably won't close them but I will try my best.

OR

Public speaking is a skill I am learning and getting great at!

I'm so looking forward to the presentation. I may be nervous—which is normal for anyone—but my confidence and knowledge of my work will quickly dissipate my nerves. I will close this new account and wow them!

Again, we have our thoughts and then we have our deep inner voice. Remember to transform both your thoughts and inner beliefs to get the best results from this system. It doesn't happen overnight, so be patient and don't give up. I've gotten to the point where I've removed all doubt and limiting beliefs from my thoughts AND from my inner-most voice. I've been practicing for at least seven years now, but saw immediately results when I first started. Some inner beliefs will be easier to change than others. Keep working at it. You can do this. You are worth it. You have a lot to accomplish and to contribute to life.

Of course there are occasions where a negative thought will try to creep in—this is normal. We are human. I am quickly able to recognize it and turn it around with a positive thought. Never let negative thoughts fester and come to anything. Dwelling and worrying is not healthy.

The outcome I strive for does not always happen either. Most times it does, but not all the time. This is normal. You must continue on with the steps and process even if things don't work out as you visualized and worked so hard to attract. Don't get discouraged or upset, as this will just bring in negative energy. Know that it will happen—it was just not the right time. Don't read into things, just keep pressing forward. Don't be too hard on yourself, but push yourself hard—there is a difference. But don't beat yourself up if things don't work out exactly how you thought they would. I always think that there is a reason that things did not work out and they will work out when it's time. This keeps me driven, excited for what's to come, and positive. Remove worry from your life. I always KNOW and BELIEVE everything will work out and there is a reason for everything— good or bad. I know that I will make it happen.

This mindset is your golden ticket to attracting everything you want in life. In the beginning, after I learned "the secret" and started building my own concepts and system, I started to see my life transform time and time again. I would visualize, believe, and achieve. Years later, it's still working for me so I know it's not just luck. It's a lifestyle, really. I just had to write this book to share with other people. Everyone should know about these principles to reach success, happiness, and more. Successful, happy people live by the principles in this book without even realizing it.

I've proven that the system works over the last seven years of my life and am grateful to be able to pass my experience on to you. The best part of this will be to hear your success stories. I know I sound like a broken record about this, but this will be so rewarding and is the true purpose of this book: to make a difference in people's lives—to make a difference in YOUR life. From big to small, I want to hear about your big dreams and your bigger achievements.

Worksheet #6

In column one, write down things you want to attract.

In column two, write down what actions you will take beyond the steps in this book to achieve your dreams.

Things you want to attract	Actions you will take beyond the steps in this book

"Do what you love smiling... enrich your life with what makes you tick."

CHAPTER 8: STEP 6—DISCOVER YOUR PASSIONS

Do you ever wonder what you are meant to be and do? The beautiful truth is that we all can do and be whatever and whoever we want, especially when following these seven steps.

Now that you have learned the steps to value yourself and know how to attract anything you want through positive thinking, your inner most beliefs, gratitude, visualization, and by taking action, the question now becomes WHAT do you want to attract? What are your big dreams?

I love every minute of my career, not just because I'm my own boss (which is a perk I am so grateful for each day) but I truly love helping businesses grow and making a positive impact on other people's lives. It's so rewarding. My husband and I started our own business together five years ago doing web design, marketing and public relations. We have four employees and are always growing. I can work twelve hours or more a day and not want to stop. My husband sometimes has to peel me away, asking for me to start dinner four or five times. I eventually do stop, and when I do, it's family time for the night—no emails and no work, just quality time with my husband. This has been key to our happiness and helps me to de-stress and not always be thinking about work. It's not healthy to be totally consumed in your work, although it's easy to do if you are a business owner or love the career that you are in. I had to learn that family is first, despite the love I have for my business.

I also like to do a brain dump every night, which I learned from positive living expert Diane Lang, who I mentioned earlier. I take a piece of paper and pen and write down everything I have to do the next day, anything that is on my mind about work, etc. Once I am done dumping it all from my brain to paper, I put the pen down and paper away. From that moment to the moment I wake up the next day, I do not think about or do any work. Of course, there are sometimes deadlines to meet, so I have to do some work, but this is generally what I do. This exercise has helped me separate owning a business with my personal and family time. My husband deserves my undivided attention; cooking dinner, eating together at the table, and cuddling on the couch watching our latest favorite shows is a routine that makes us closer and happy. I never go to bed with my mind racing with thoughts of work, which means I fall asleep quickly. The next day—only after I go through my gratitude list, eat a healthy breakfast, and drink two glasses of water—I revisit work and start my day, starting with Brendon Burchard's Productivity Worksheet and Rachel Luna's Confidentiality Worksheet. I end up being much more productive and less stressed by taking time for family at night.

So what makes you tick? What do you love to do? Think in detail exactly what your ideal relationship, career, social life, and overall lifestyle looks like. Use these seven steps to be who you want to be—and don't hold back! I always like to ask people, "What are you good at?" Is it cleaning, organizing, putting outfits together, baking, or helping people? Whatever it is, know what makes you happy and identify what you are good at.

VentureMom.com is an amazing resource for moms who want to start their own business venture. In Holly Hurd's new book, *Venture Mom: From Idea to Income in Just 12 Weeks*, she shares how to decide on your passion—a business idea. She says to think about what other people say you are good at. For example, do people always say that you have the best style and outfits, you make the best lasagna, or you are such a people person, etc.? These are clues to discover your true passions. By the way, Holly's book is really for anyone, not just moms. I recommend you read it!

Worksheet #7

List the things you are good at and answer these three questions:

- What hobbies do you enjoy?

- What activities make you happy?

- What do other people say you are good at?

Hobbies I Enjoy

1. _____

2. _____

3. _____

4. _____

5. _____

6. _____

7. _____

Activities That Make Me Happy

1. _____

2. _____

3. _____

4. _____

5. _____

6. _____

7. _____

Other People Say I'm Good at...

1. _____

2. _____

3. _____

4. _____

5. _____

6. _____

7. _____

Sometimes we cannot immediately do what we love as a full-time career, but this is okay. Use these steps to attract the money-making business/career that you love. If whatever job or career you are in now is not your first choice, visualize your ideal career and attract this to be your reality.

While in college, I worked three jobs. I woke up at or before five o'clock in the morning and went to this musty basement office to work at an answering service, taking calls and messages for businesses outside of working hours. I remember the pay was low and the mold in the office made me sick within an hour of being there. Within thirty minutes of leaving, I would feel better, but I was grateful to have the job that put extra money in my pocket. My second job was another part-time position, working a few days a week as a residential home appraiser apprentice. This was exciting, challenging, and I learned a lot. My main job was at an inbound call center as a direct response marketing representative; we sold weight loss products and things like natural Viagra-type products. This paid my way through community college. Back then, I did not realize I was doing it, but I was using some of the concepts in this book to make great sales numbers and become one of the top ten agents in the company. When I arrived at my cubicle (more like a phone cubby), I would write down my sales goals for the day and truly believe that I would have amazing sales that day. I enjoyed working there and it was a perfect job while I was in college.

After college, I started working at a law firm and some insurance companies until I opened my own marketing and public relations firm—the best decision I ever made. So my point is, it's okay to be in a job or career that is not your ideal dream—everyone starts somewhere. Use these seven steps to change your reality. Be patient, work hard, and keep following the system. This system works. Sometimes, depending on your dream, it takes weeks, months, or maybe years if it's something really major, but I have had things manifest in just days before. Just believe and know it will happen, and rid your inner voice of all doubt.

Everyone has a purpose in this world, and we can all contribute to making it a better world to live in. That's why Step 1 of valuing yourself is so integral to the entire process taught in this book. You can do whatever you want; never lose sight of this. Don't get discouraged. Remember: if you want it, reach out and grab it. It's yours!

From a young age, I wanted to be successful and knew that I

would be one day. I grew up with my mom working three jobs to make ends meet. This motivated me to be successful so I could give back to my mom and repay her for everything she has done and worked so hard for. At the age of fifteen, I would tell my mom, "You wait, mom; I will make you so proud by doing great things." She recently shared this story with me, followed by how proud she is today of the woman I have become. She continued on and shared that she looks up to me, respects me, and that I help her live a positive life.

Hearing these words means more than I can describe. My mom is my rock, and I am the women I am today because of her. I'm so fortunate to have a mom like her. I put her through so much worry in my teen years when I veered off the path. I always wanted to make up for putting her in this situation—causing her undeserved pain, worry, and stress. Now, I finally feel like I am making up for those years. Not knowing if your daughter is dead in a ditch somewhere is a terrifying way to go to sleep each night. No mother should go through this.

So what are you passions? A good way to determine your passions is to write a list of everything you enjoy doing—even if it's fantasy football, write it down. You never know where a great idea will come from. Your aptitude for statistics could land you a great career you love or you could even coach a college football team!

My work is a huge part of my passion, but it's important to have passion outside of work in other areas of life:

- Hobbies

- Socializing

- Family

- Exercise

- Food

- Learning

- Traveling

- Love

Add to the list as you see fit. Determine your passions within each of these categories to really expand your life and achieve complete joy and abundance.

I'll be the first one to admit that my business is number one, and I spend a lot of time on this passion. Balance is a must, though, so I make time for all the other great prongs of life. I love to travel, for example. I use these seven steps to attract travel to our lives. My uncle always goes to five-star resorts, so I started planning a trip to our first five-star resort in the Dominican Republic. This would cost a pretty penny—over $5K for eight days—but I believed that it would be possible, used all seven steps, and took action to make it happen! It was a beautiful trip for our anniversary and came at the perfect time—before we got pregnant. We have travelled each year of our marriage, two to three times a year on cruises or resorts, to Russia each year, and more. All this is possible because I believe it to be. You want to bask in the sun on a warm, Caribbean beach? You want to see the world? You want to take a road trip from coast to coast? Use these seven steps to attract exactly this, and please share photos with us on Facebook and tell us about your travels! The proof is in the pudding, as the saying goes, so when you start seeing results, we want to hear about it.

I also love trying new restaurants; farm-to-table is my favorite type of place. My best friend and I often meet for lunch to indulge in great food, a glass of good, red wine (before I was pregnant), and inspiring conversation with lots of smiles (and some selfies). These social moments bring such joy and balance to my life. Identifying passions outside of just work actually helps me be more productive in my business, which leads to more success. Being happy in many areas of life is best.

Worksheet #8

List as many passions as you can think of—things you enjoy doing for all or some of the categories below:

- Hobbies

- Socializing

- Family

- Exercise

- Food

- Learning

- Traveling

- Love

- Career

My Passions

1. _____

2. _____

3. _____

4. _____

5. _____

6. _____

7. _____

8. _____

9. _____

10. _____

Build your dreams off your passions for ultimate happiness and success.

"Random acts of kindness boosts our happiness. Be kind even when no one is looking."

CHAPTER 9: STEP 7—PAY IT FORWARD

This last step rounds out the system of how to truly attract anything you want. Paying it forward so others can experience the complete joy and abundance that you do is the best feeling. I truly believe the world will be a better place if we follow these seven steps. When we are happy, we can make others around us happy. It's a chain reaction, really.

When we feel fulfilled, we strive to achieve more. This is why I wrote this book—to pay if forward two-fold:

To teach to you and others the seven steps that have transformed my life, giving anyone the ability to dream big and achieve bigger. To give you the tools to feel complete joy, happiness, success, and more. This system is a gift that everyone should be given.

To thank, mention, and give gratitude to those who have impacted me along the way. The shout-outs in this book are not paid advertisements, and I was not asked to promote anyone. It's me wanting to share with you the people who have helped me. I truly recommend them as resources.

I often buy the book, *The Secret*, by Rhonda Byrne and send it to people as a gift. I am so excited to share what I learned with others. If you enjoyed this book and especially when the principles taught in it start working for you, I would be so grateful to know that you are paying it forward by telling others about your experience with this book—and even giving it as a gift! What better gift to give than the tools to help one attract the life they dream about. It's pretty cool if you were the one who started the process for them. This is how I looked at it when I gifted the book, *The Secret*, many times over the years. For me, to pass on this knowledge and see someone transform their life is the best feeling. The gratitude that they have for me sharing these principles with them is life-long. It's the one thing we can do to make a huge, lasting, positive impact on someone.

I also wanted to talk about random acts of kindness. Deep inside, I believe that good things happen to good people. By completing random acts of kindness—whether it's sending someone a book with a handwritten note, taking someone to lunch, paying for someone's groceries, donating money when asked at stores during checkout, opening the door, or even a simple smile or compliment—I am able to accelerate these seven steps and my internal magnet becomes stronger. I do these random acts of kindness to help others, not for motivation to help myself—the benefits to me are simply a great by-product that occurs. Not to mention, completing a random act of kindness boosts your happiness for at least twenty-four hours! Thank you, Diane Lang, for teaching me this. (www.dlcounseling.com)

We want to make it easy for you to pay it forward, so here's a gift from us. Visit www.achievebigger.com/gift to check for special offers for any copy of this book you gift to others.

We are paying it forward in another exciting way too! I know we shared this in the beginning, but it bears mention again. We created a non-profit called The Dream Fund, where a portion of the book proceeds are donated.

We will give grant money (free with no strings attached) to help people achieve their dreams. Just visit www.achievebigger.com/dream-fund to submit your story and tell us what your dream is. You tell us how much money you need to get started, and whether it's $100, $1,000, $10,000, or more, we will choose as many people as possible to reward grants to. The more books we sell, the more people we help. This is our most important mission. You can help out by going to www.achievebigger.com/share to share this book on social media and via email. We made it super easy, taking only one click!

My Pay It Forward List:

Here are some of the many people who have helped, supported, and inspired me along the way:

My mother, Micheline Mayberry: Mom, you are the best mom a child could dream of. You taught me so many amazing values and shaped me into the woman I am today. Thank you for all that you have done. Your kindness, generosity, and love are second to none. You deserve all the best in this world. I have eternal gratitude to you and love you more than my words can describe.

Rachel Luna: Rachel, you have inspired me for years and I love your Facebook posts on your page, https://www.facebook.com/RachelLunaTV! You are so strong, balancing your own business and family. I loved hearing you speak and meeting you at the Spark & Hustle conference in New York City. You are electric and your energy is contagious. Your Confidence worksheet is so helpful (get it here: http://b7lzq4lt.megaph.com/) and I LOVE, LOVE, LOVE your book, *Successful People are Full of C.R.A.P. Courage, Resilience, Authenticity, Perseverance.* I recommend anyone reading this to read your book! Keep being the amazing you that you are!

Learn more about Rachel Luna and her amazing coaching services at http://rachelluna.biz/ .

Adriana Taverez: Adriana, you are my best friend and entrepreneur bestie, too! From the moment I met you, your energy and spirit impacted me. Through your support, wisdom, coaching, and more I have grown as a person. Thank you for all that you have done as a friend and a business creator. I'm excited to continue to work with you on many projects! Thank you for being a true friend—love you!

Adriana has been called among her clients "transformation miracle worker" for her ability to assist others in releasing destructive emotions and/or behavioral patterns affecting all areas of their life. Her 15 years' experience in nutritional coaching, personal development, and stress management techniques give her a uniquely broad perspective on integrative coaching. With clients ranging from individuals seeking weight loss to businesses seeking leadership interventions, Adriana brings an unusually wide range of experience to her coaching practice.

To learn more about Adriana, visit www.facebook.com/HealthCoachSecrets.

Karen Koslov-Barski: My dearest, Karen! We met almost ten years ago, and I've been grateful ever since to know such a beautiful, amazing woman, inside and out. Do you know that you were the one who turned my life around when introducing me to the book, *The Secret*, and showing me, through your amazing life, just how powerful it is to attract anything you want? I am eternally grateful to you and will always admire your strength, positivity, and total conviction in being your true self and making dreams come true. You have such a beautiful family and I'm excited for Pasha and I to start our family. Keep inspiring and doing what you do best. I am excited for you to write your book!

Karen is the owner and founder of the amazing baby swaddle brand, Woombie. If you have a baby on the way or a new baby at home, the Woombie is a must-have to promote healthy, safe sleep for the entire family. Learn more at http://www.woombie.com.

Brendon Burchard: Brendon, I took your *Total Product Blueprint* course and it was amazing! You immediately resonated with me, and your energy is infectious. Since the course, I have used the strategies you taught over and over again; they work wonderfully! Thank you for being so inspirational and helping so many people achieve great success. I love all your books, and *The Charge* was especially awesome.

You are so real and just a good person, which always shines through. I am impressed with your story, and you will continue to inspire me forever.

Brendon Burchard is a self-made multi-millionaire who helps businesses and entrepreneurs achieve their highest dreams through blogs, videos, programs, books, and more. Visit http://brendon.com to find out more.

Jeff Walker: Jeff, the very first time I watched one of your videos, I was hooked. Your realness and passion to help people touches me greatly, and I want to thank you for everything you have taught me and for inspiring and motivating millions of people. I LOVE, LOVE, LOVE your book, *Launch*. I highly recommend everyone to purchase this book. Thank you for all that you have given to me.

Jeff Walker, the creator of the *Product Launch Formula*, a system that's been used by thousands of entrepreneurs in hundreds of different niches and markets to create hugely successful product launches. The impact has been crazy huge…his students and clients have now done well over $500 million in product launches. Jeff Walker's book, *Launch*, is a must read. Along the way, he's coached or helped all kinds of experts such as Tony Robbins, Brendon Burchard, Dan Kennedy, Bill Glazer, Rich Schefren, Frank Kern, Dean Graziosi, Yanik Silver, Greg Clement and dozens more "gurus" — but Jeff get smost excited about all of the "regular folks" that he has helped quit their jobs and grow serious businesses. Learn more at www.jeffwalker.com.

Rhonda Byrne—author of *The Secret*: Rhonda, what a

masterpiece! *The Secret* and all your other books are MUST, MUST reads. You changed my life in too many ways to list, so I will just say thank you from the bottom of my heart. The work you do to inspire others and change their lives by complete empowerment is a mission I share. I will rave about *The Secret* forever and it's one of my favorite gifts to give. I give gratitude each day for being introduced to your book. Thank you.

Rhonda Byrne is the creator and Executive Producer of the film *The Secret*, and Author of the books *The Secret*, *The Power*, *The Magic*, and *Hero*. Learn more at http://www.thesecret.tv.

Diane Lang: Diane, you are my favorite positive living expert and coach! You do amazing work and have taught me so much about happiness and balance in my life. Your book, *Creating Balance and Finding Happiness*, helped me so much. Thank you. Keep on rockin' it. I will be forever grateful.

Diane Lang is a Therapist, Educator, Author and Coach with an expertise in multiple mental health, lifestyle and parenting needs. Her books are a must read! Learn more at www.dlcounseling.com.

Marla the *Fly Lady*: Marla, one conversation was all it took to be touched by you! We spoke on the phone for 1.5 hours (thank you for taking the time to chat!). You truly inspired me after learning about your self-published books; especially the 40,000 copies sold of your first. You are a true pillar of inspiration to me and many others (your million followers says something!). I could immediately tell how special you are and I feel privileged to have met you. I love your Facebook page (www.facebook.com/TheFlyLady); I get great dinner ideas! Let's have more empowering conversations; I am grateful to be acquainted.

Do you feel overwhelmed, overextended, and overdrawn? The Fly Lady is here to help you through housecleaning and organizing tips with homespun humor, daily musings about life and love, the Sidetracked Home Executives (SHE) system, and anything else that is on her mind.

When you join FlyLady, you will receive daily FLYmail. Your FLYing Lessons will guide you through baby steps to help you set up routines, get rid of your clutter, and put your home and life in order. FlyLady's approach has worked for thousands. Join anytime you want (there is no cost involved)! Visit http://www.flylady.net to sign up and for more information.

My beautiful sister, Karen Cookson: Karen, it seems so long ago that we were having sleepovers at dad's house taking turns tickling each other's arms before bed. You have become a beacon of light in my life. I am grateful and fortunate to have a sister like you. Your kind words, compassionate and encouraging text messages, unconditional love, non-judgmental character, positive outlook on life, and strong will to do the next best/right thing truly make me a better person. We laugh alike, we think alike, we are sisters connected forever as we journey through this amazing life. I love you and can truly say you are a true friend in addition to being my beautiful, vibrant sister.

My husband and best friend, Pavel Mullyakaev: Pasha, I did it! I know I've been talking to you for many years about my dream to write this book. Thank you for listening and encouraging me to finish! We live together, own a business together, and work at home together (on top of both being Leos)…we get along like best friends and never get sick of each other. I'm so proud of us; still going strong after five years of wonderful marriage. Each day gets better and better.

When I first met you I knew you were my match. I'm so grateful to be loved so much by you, and as we start our new chapter of parenthood, I'm overfilled with joy and have big dreams for our family. Together, we can make anything happen.

Our beautiful, smart, and healthy baby boy will be born soon – our creation from pure love. I love you more than words can describe here on this page. I love making our dreams come true with you. You are my forever soul mate. Ya lublu tebya.

Saint Mary's Rehab: To the staff of Saint Mary's Rehab and Dr. Treworgy, over 15 years ago I was a patient in your detox/inpatient rehab program. I waited 10 hours in the waiting room to get a bed. I remember being scared, but hopeful as I finally took the first step to put my life back on the right path. The very first night I was fearful thinking, "How will I get through this first night with withdrawals?" But something miraculous happened. As the ward was quiet and dark with everyone nestled in their beds, I lay there awake. I looked out the window and saw a glow of light all around the cross that sits upon the roof of the hospital. I rubbed my eyes and looked again. Was it tired eyes playing tricks on me? The big glow around the cross was still there! I immediately felt comforted and knew I would get through the first night. I even was able to sleep the entire night until morning. (Each night after I looked out the window to try to catch the glowing cross again, but I never saw it again. The beautiful cross was the only thing I saw.)

As each day (each hour) went on while staying in your facility, I learned so much about addiction and about myself. I felt secure, safe, and in control for the first time in a long time. Of course many emotions were surfacing and it was not easy, but I am proud to say I've been drug-free for over a decade and St. Mary's was the start of it.

I am grateful for your program, your staff, and my amazing doctor. The sessions, activities, speakers, and more were life-changing…heck, even the food was great! I even went through your 30-day intensive outpatient program where I was told I left as a beautiful butterfly because of how much I transformed and grew. This was exactly how I felt.

So I wanted to write this note of gratitude and share that today I am drug-free; an owner of a six-figure, self-made business; married to the love of my life with a baby on the way; closing on our first home, have no debt (aside from student loans) with an excellent credit score, free of anxiety and panic attacks without the use of medication, I love life no matter what comes my way…and much more. Thank you for helping me find my way and for helping everyone else who has laid their head down in St. Mary's rehab. Continue doing great work and know you are making beautiful, positive, lasting change in the lives of many. I am eternally grateful.

Worksheet #9

Share your pay it forward list; those who influence you, support you…those who simply love you.

My Pay It Forward List

1. _____

2. _____

3. _____

4. _____

5. _____

6. _____

7. _____

8. _____

9. _____

10. _____

Next, write down ideas for random acts of kindness; choose one a month or one a week to complete.

Random Acts of Kindness Ideas

1. _____

2. _____

3. _____

4. _____

5. _____

6. _____

7. _____

8. _____

9. _____

10. _____

"Dream BIG.
Achieve BIGGER."

CHAPTER 10: FINAL WORDS

Thank you from the bottom of my heart for taking the time to read my book. It's my first book and I look forward to feedback and especially stories of success. I've wanted to write this book for a few years now and am grateful that it's complete. This is not just a book, but a community of support for you. We are here to help you dream big and achieve bigger. We are here to lift you to your highest dreams and achievements. We are here to believe in you.

I always love to hear from fans, so please email me at tasha@achievebigger.com for anything you need or want to share.

Now that you have read the book, it's time to put these steps into practice. It may be a lot to take in, but go back and reference the material once and awhile to brush up. Eventually, these steps will become second nature and a part of your way of living.

As I said throughout this book, no matter where you have been in life and where you are now—from feeling completely down and out with no options, to being super successful and happy—this book offers tools to dig deep and find your true self, motivation, and purpose. When we are happy and successful, we impact those around us to be the same, causing a beautiful chain reaction of encouragement and positivity.

As I start a new, thrilling chapter of my life by entering into motherhood, I am excited to pass on these principles to my children. Seeing them blossom from a young age will be so fulfilling to witness. Yes, I've made mistakes, but I've certainly learned from these mistakes and now have more tools to pass down to the next generation. It's almost like I will get to relive my child and teen years through my children; what a cool experience to parent and impact the path of your kids' lives.

I close this book with these final words:

Thank you. I am grateful that you are reading these words. You can do and be anything in this great life. Build your foundation of good values, truly value yourself, and remove all limiting beliefs—even the ones deep within. Turn all thoughts to positive ones, have gratitude each day for what has happened and what will happen, visualize success, amplify the law of attraction by taking action, discover your passions to create joy in all facets of life, and pay it forward to share your experience with others so everyone can feel as great as you. If you want something, reach out and grab it!

Warmest regards. Let's connect on social media! And remember… Dream BIG, achieve BIGGER!

ABOUT THE AUTHOR

Tasha L. Mayberry

Entrepreneur, Wife, Mom & Life's Biggest Fan

Growing up in Windham, Maine raised by an amazing mother gave me a memorable, happy childhood. It was effortless for me to get straight A's in school even in honors classes. With the world as my oyster to make beautiful pearls, there seemed to be no stopping me, an ambitious girl with dreams as big as the sky… BUT a few bad choices and wrong turns led to years of substance abuse in my late teens. This part

119

of my life I have learned does not define me, yet it helped shape me into the woman I am today.

By my early 20's I was drug-free and on a path of self-discovery learning so much about my true self and purpose. A turning point in my life was when I read the book, *The Secret*, by Rhonda Byrne, a philosophy based on using positive thinking, gratitude and the law of attract to make any dream a reality. For seven years, I have practiced a set of 7 steps that I created to achieve a life full of abundance, happiness, and success.

Where I was years ago seems to be a universe away from where I am today. From a stagnant life paralyzed by substance-abuse, living paycheck to paycheck, having bad credit, gaining 40 pounds at one point, suffering from severe anxiety and panic attacks, being in dead-end relationships, to NOW…being drug-free for over a decade, owning a six-figure, self-made business, excellent credit score, savings in the bank, healthy and fit, no longer suffering from anxiety or panic attacks without the use of medication, married to the love of my life with a baby on the way, and loving life no matter what comes my way.

It's not magic. It's not luck. I created all of this by following a simple set of seven steps. I now gift these steps to you.

www.ingramcontent.com/pod-product-compliance
Lightning Source LLC
Chambersburg PA
CBHW031535040426
42445CB00010B/554